# Colors with Samsoon

## Korean Learning & Coloring (Vol. 3)

*samsoon adventures*

samsoon adventures 🌸

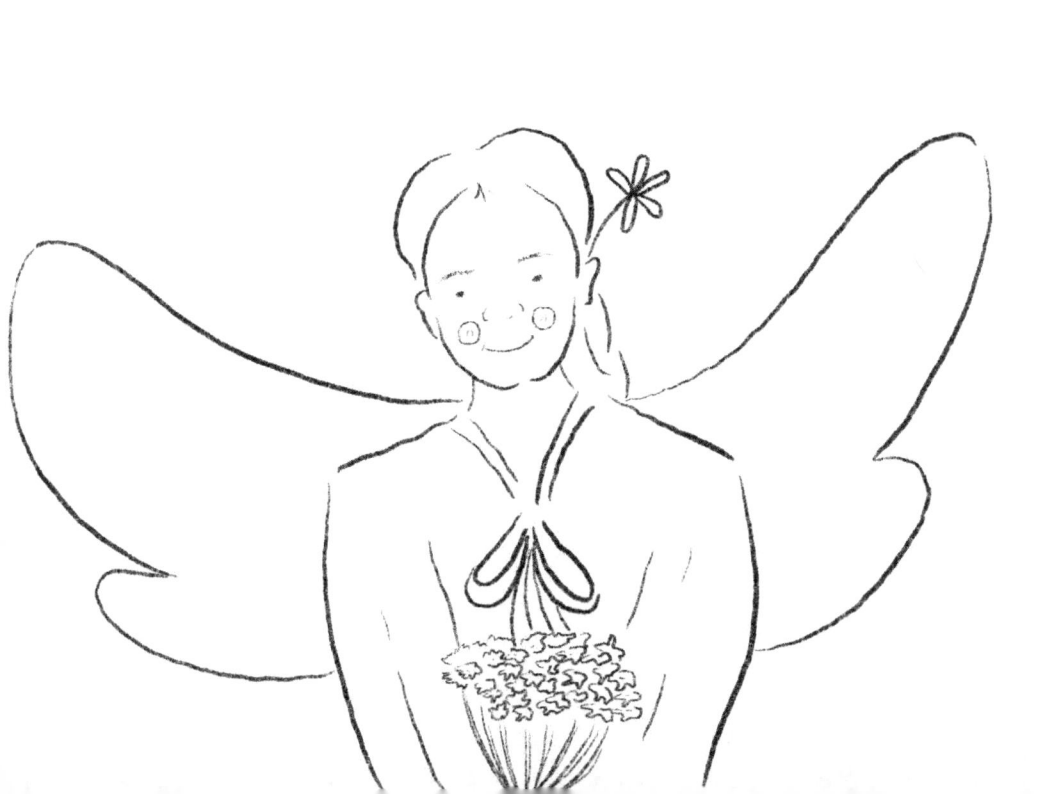

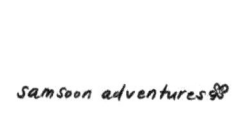
samsoon adventures

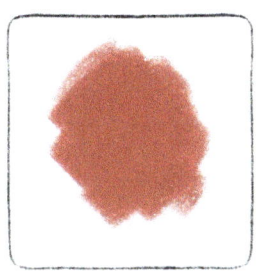

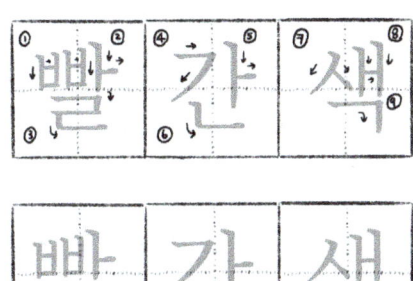

(ppal-gaan-saek)
red

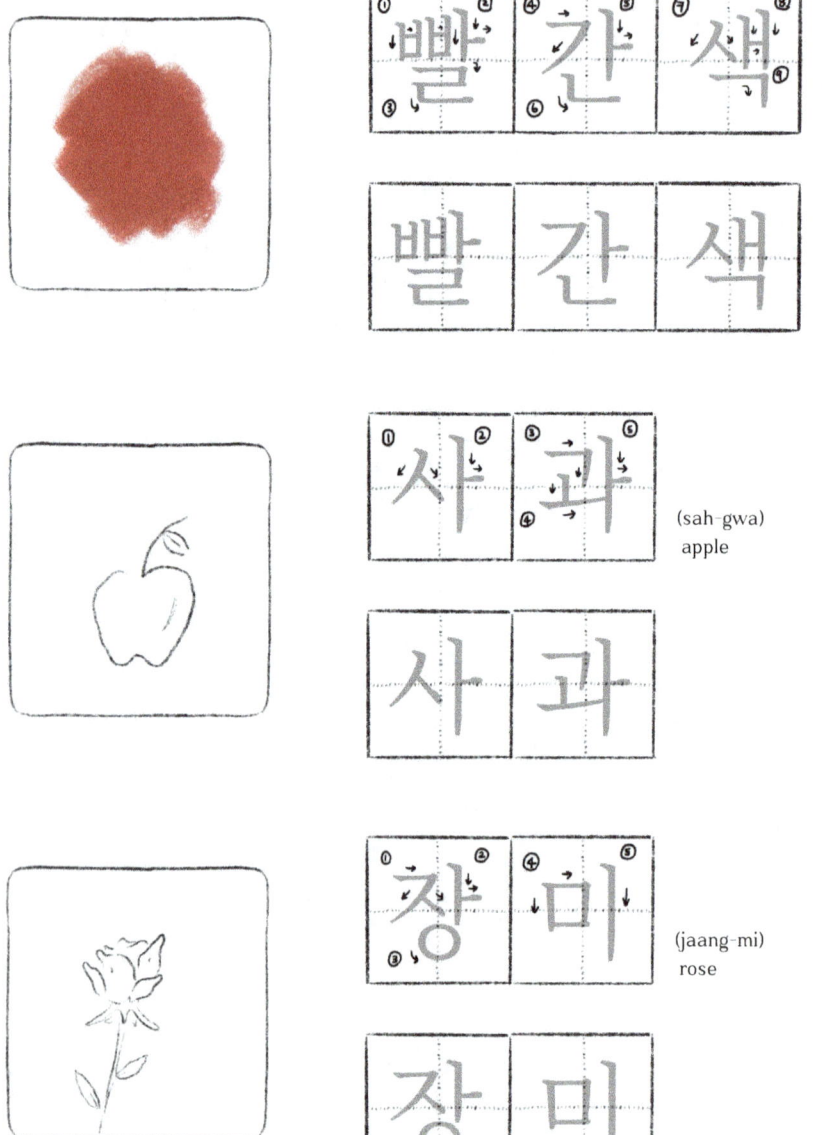

빨 간 색 (ppal-gaan-saek) red

빨 간 색

사 과 (sah-gwa) apple

사 과

장 미 (jaang-mi) rose

장 미

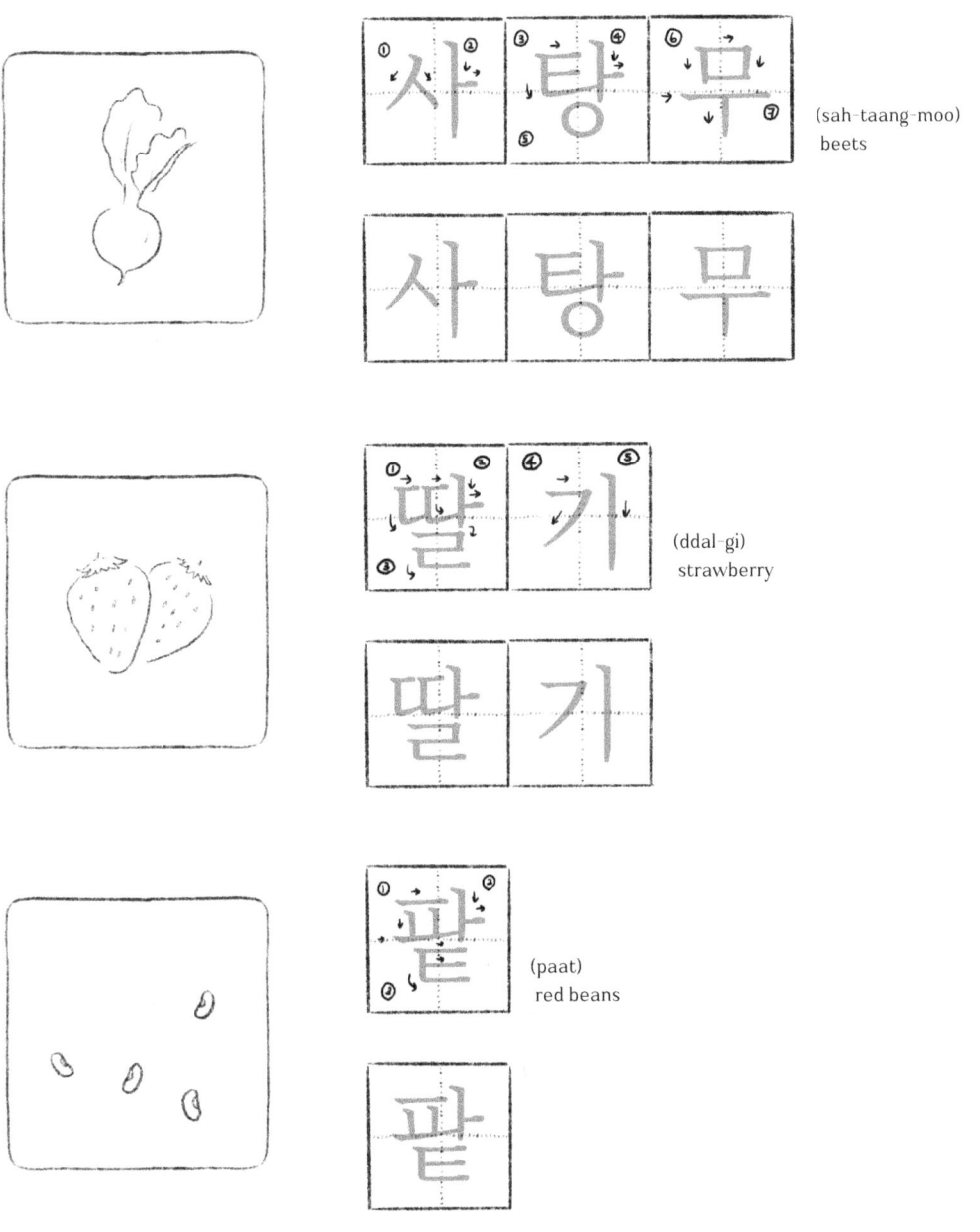

(sah-taang-moo)
beets

(ddal-gi)
strawberry

(paat)
red beans

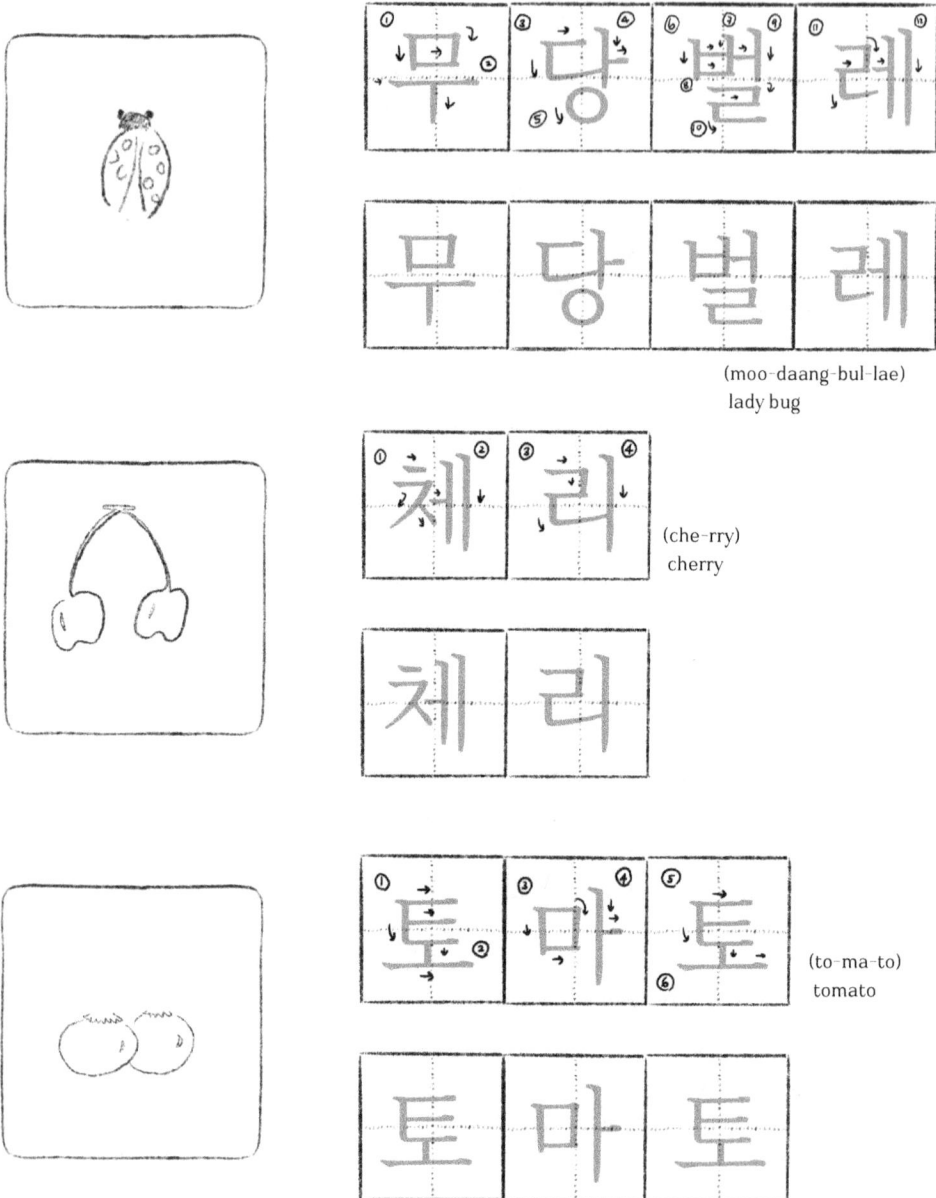

무 당 벌 레

(moo-daang-bul-lae)
lady bug

체 리

(che-rry)
cherry

토 마 토

(to-ma-to)
tomato

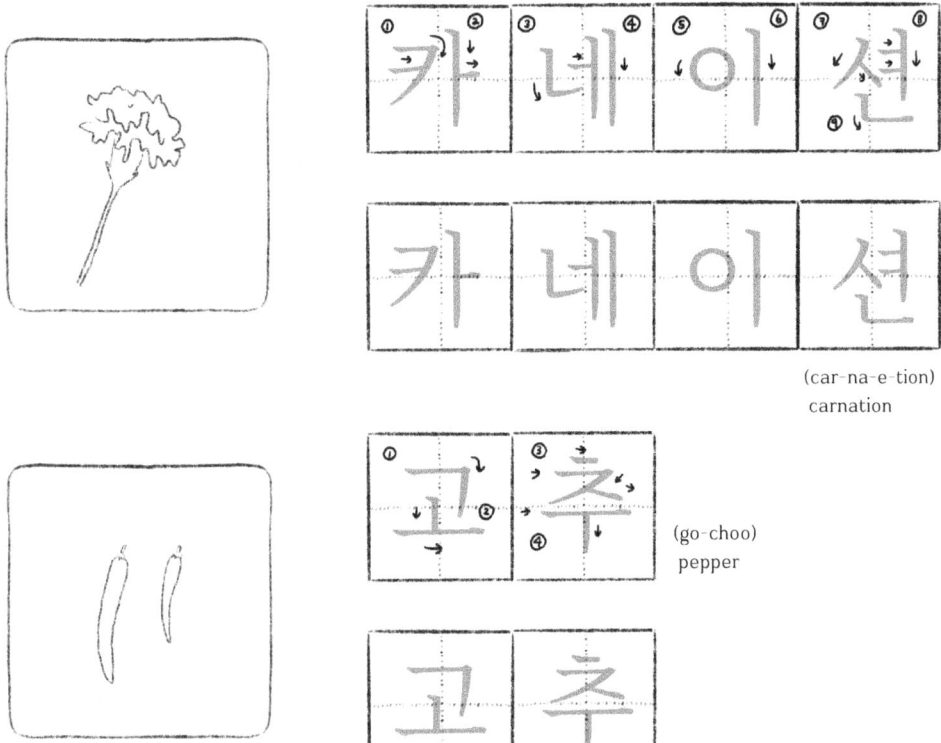

카 네 이 션

(car-na-e-tion)
carnation

고 추

(go-choo)
pepper

samsoon adventures 🐾

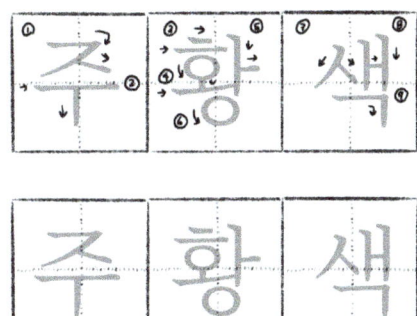

(joo-hwang-saek)
orange

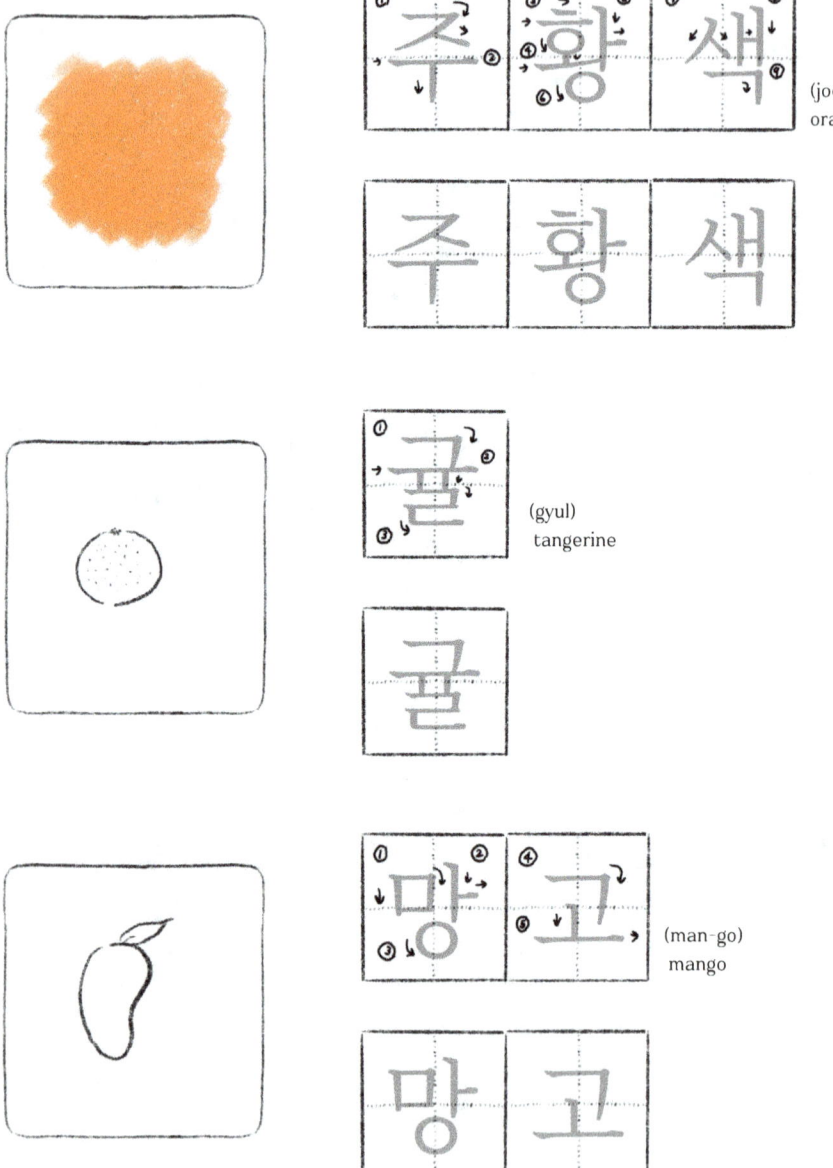

주황색
(joo-hwang-saek)
orange

귤
(gyul)
tangerine

망고
(man-go)
mango

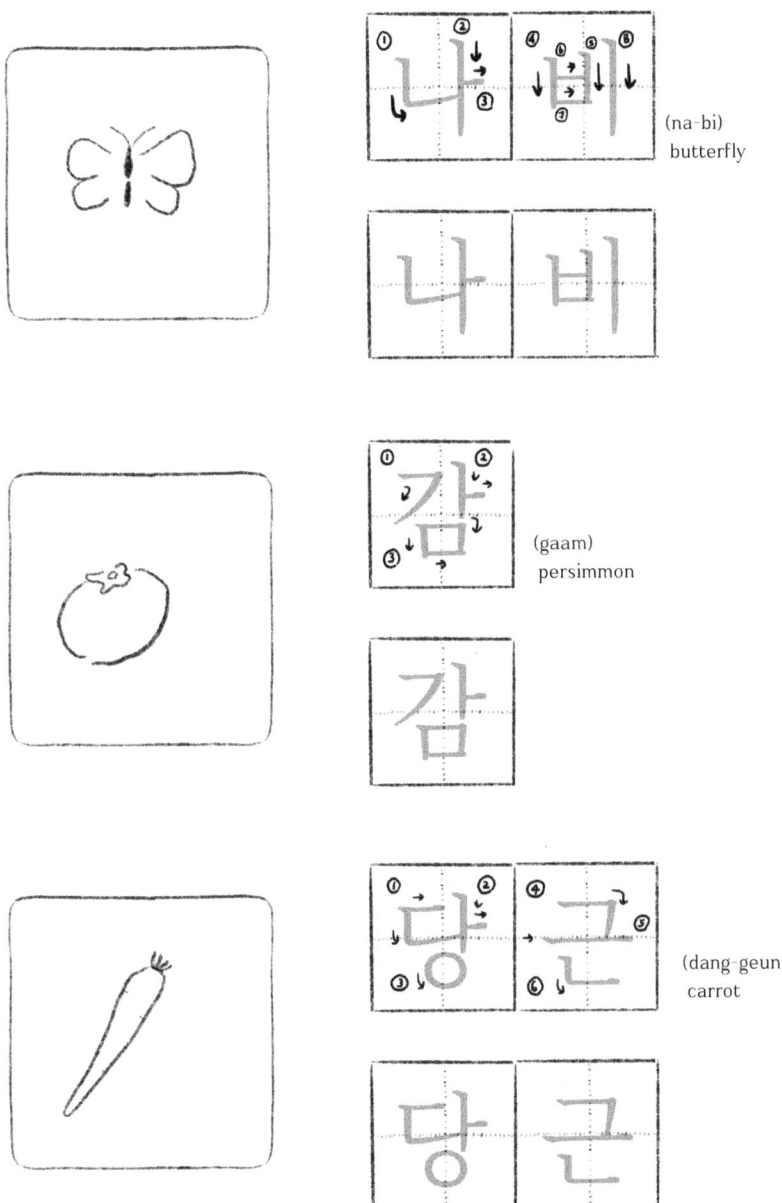

(na-bi)
butterfly

(gaam)
persimmon

(dang-geun)
carrot

samsoon adventures ✿

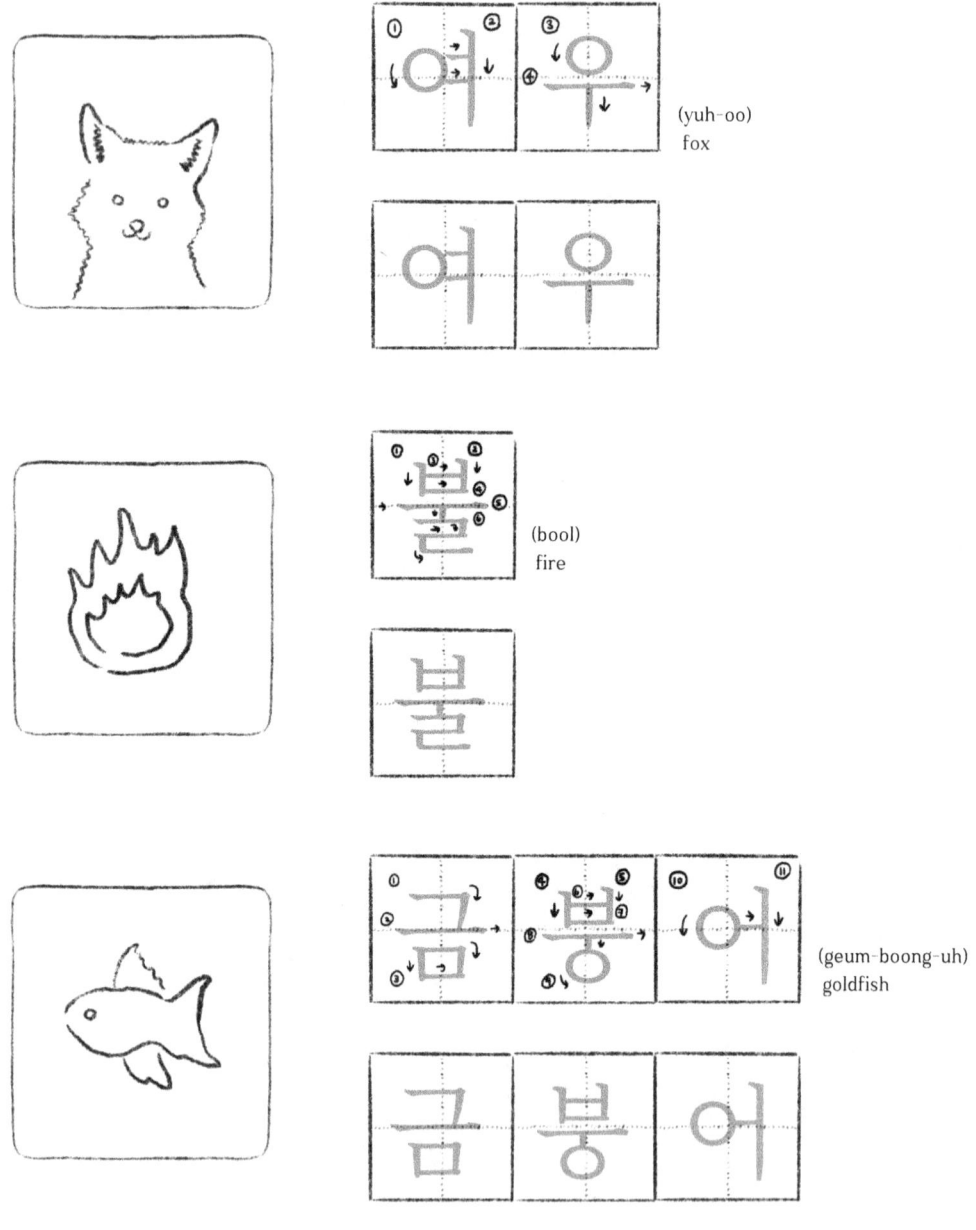

(yuh-oo)
fox

(bool)
fire

(geum-boong-uh)
goldfish

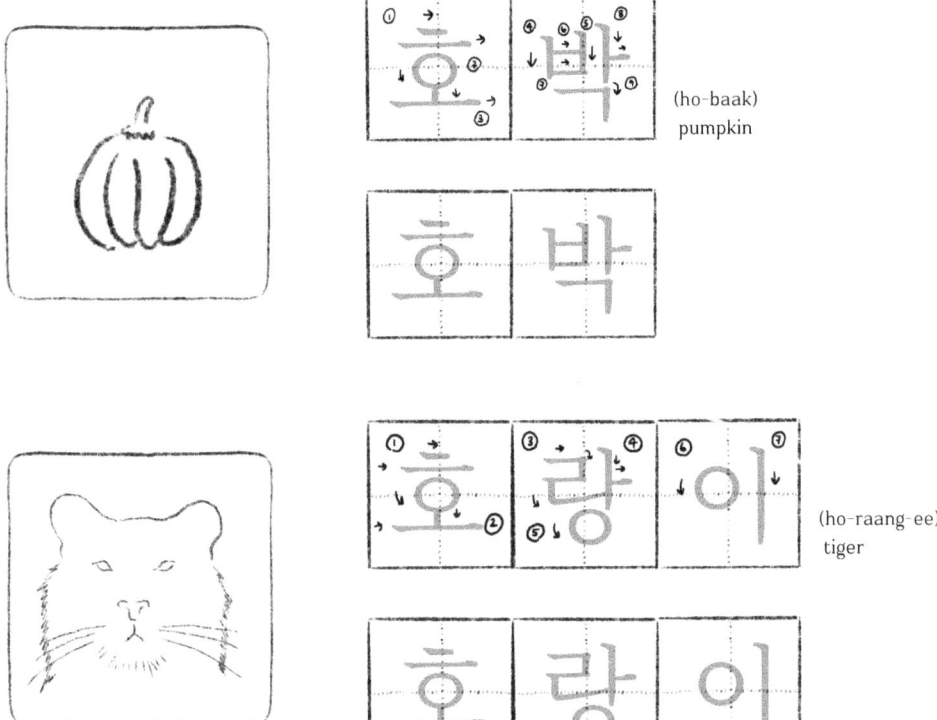

(ho-baak)
pumpkin

(ho-raang-ee)
tiger

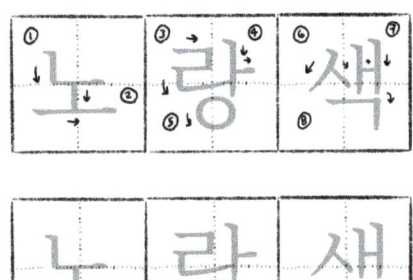

(noh-raang-saek)
yellow

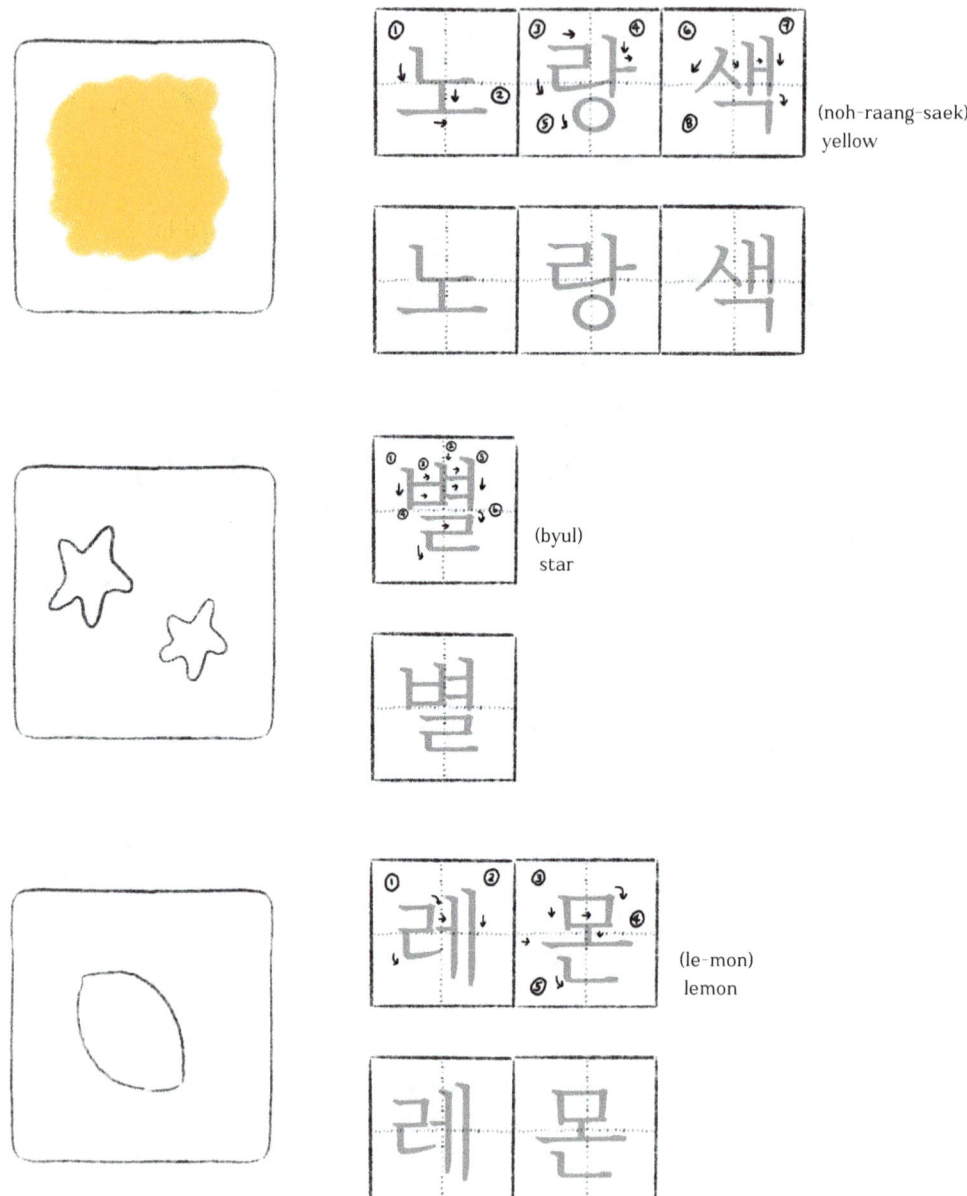

(noh-raang-saek)
yellow

노랑색

(byul)
star

별

(le-mon)
lemon

레몬

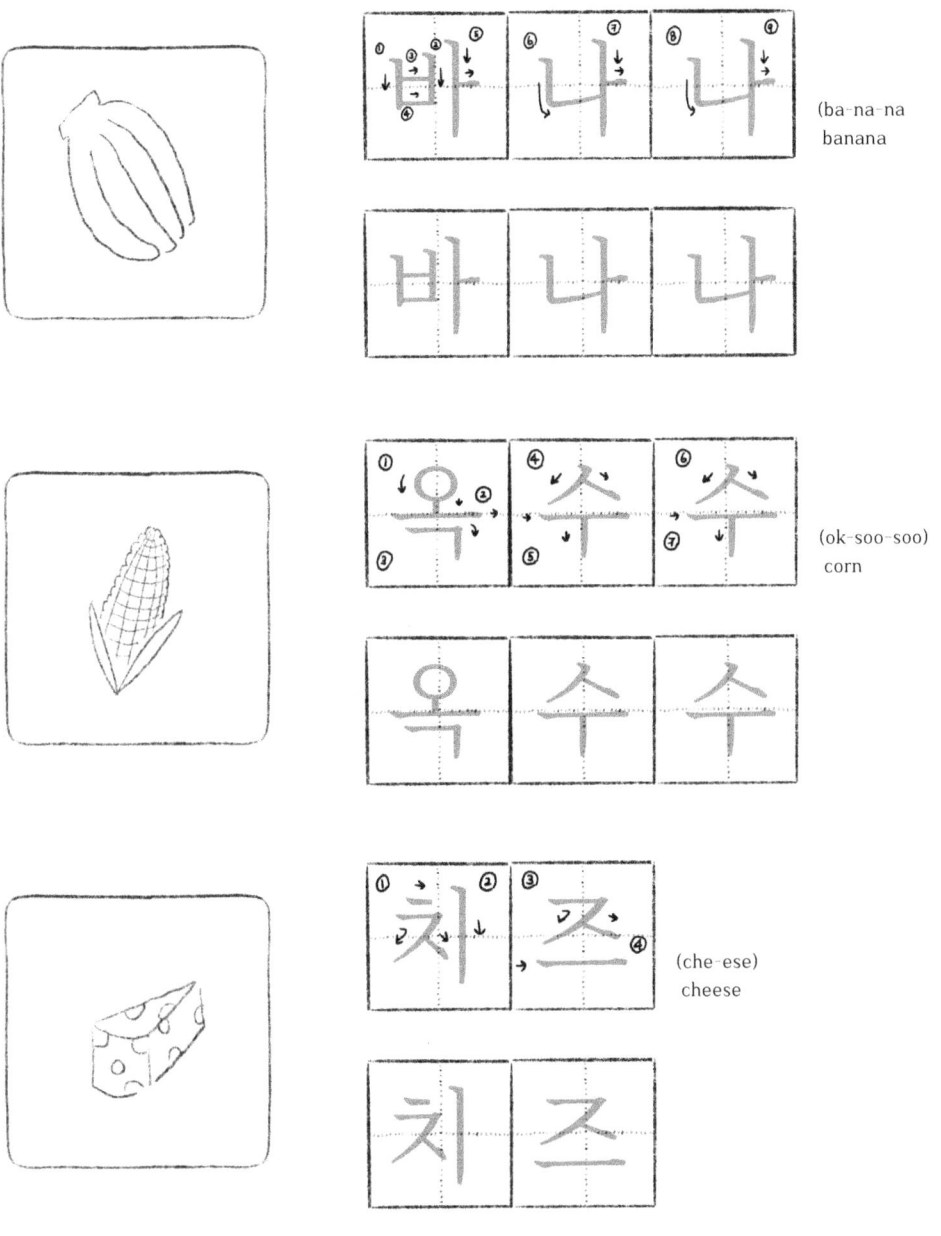

(ba-na-na)
banana

(ok-soo-soo)
corn

(che-ese)
cheese

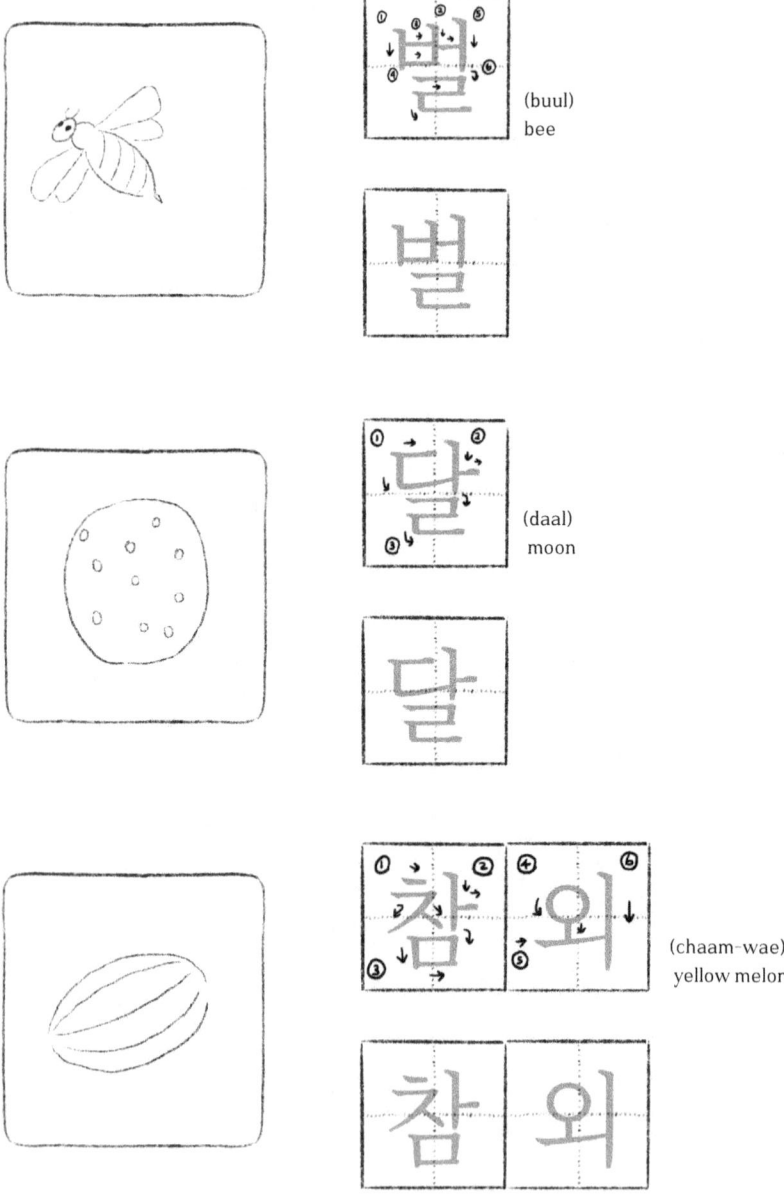

(buul)
bee

(daal)
moon

(chaam-wae)
yellow melon

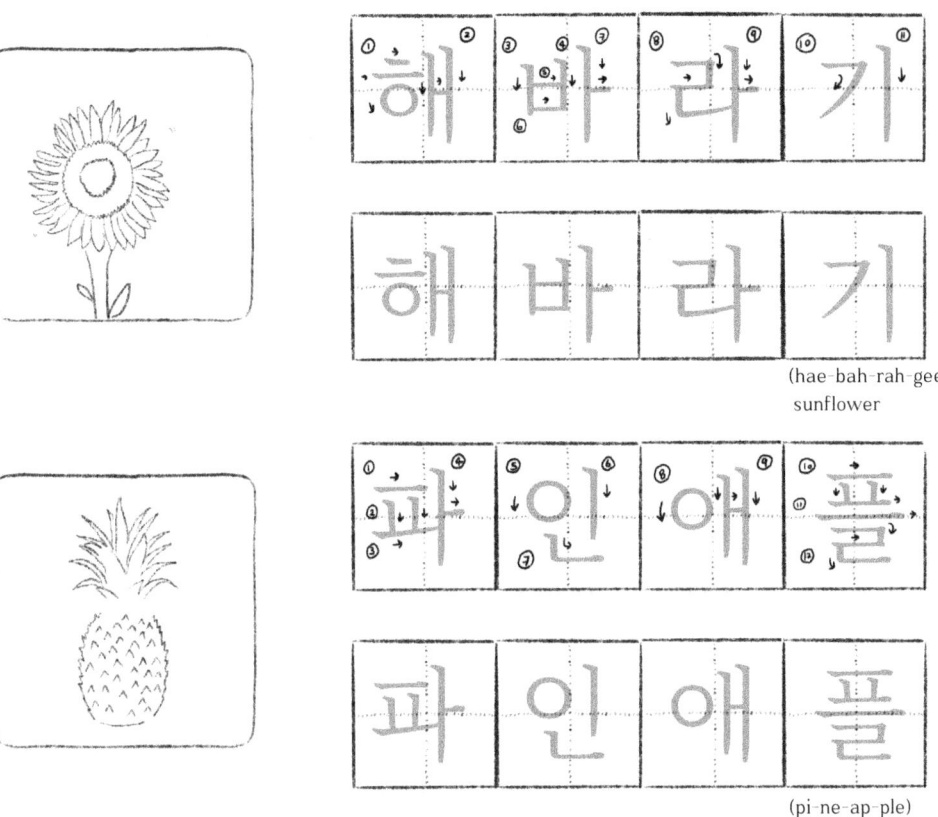

(hae-bah-rah-gee)
sunflower

(pi-ne-ap-ple)
pineapple

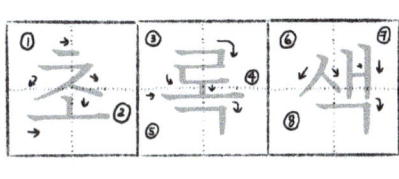

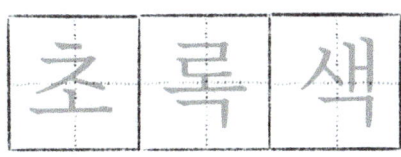

(cho-rok-saek)

green

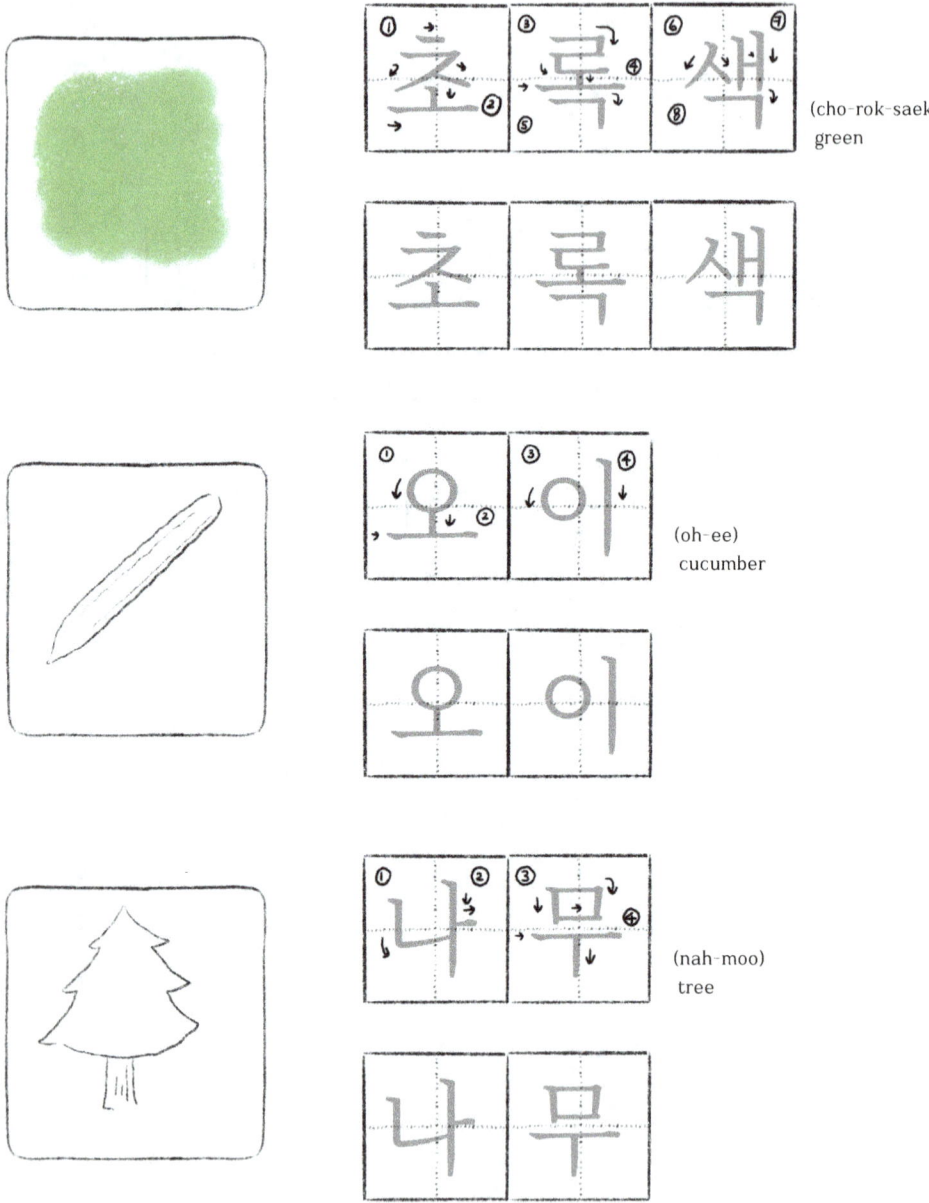

초록색 (cho-rok-saek) green

오이 (oh-ee) cucumber

나무 (nah-moo) tree

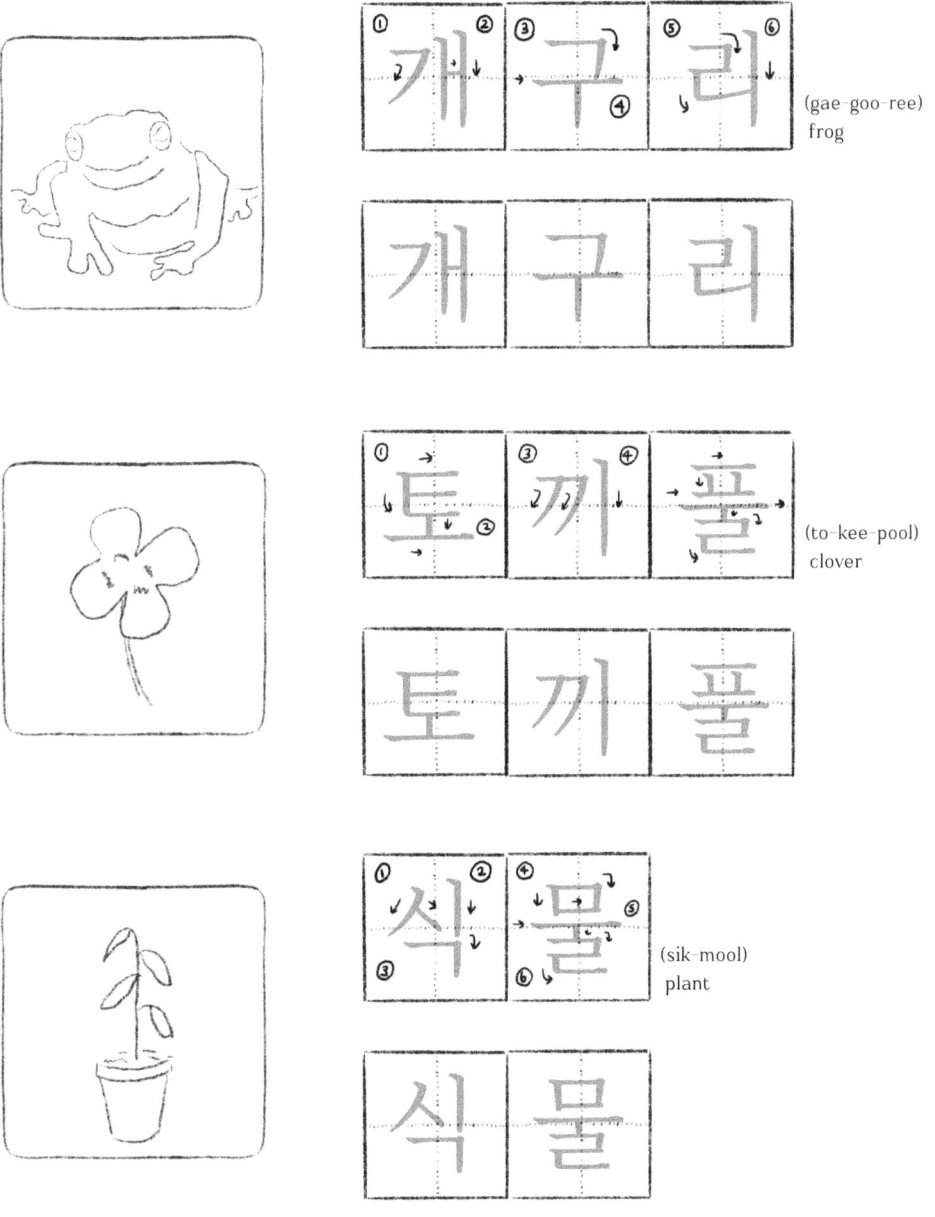

(gae-goo-ree)
frog

(to-kee-pool)
clover

(sik-mool)
plant

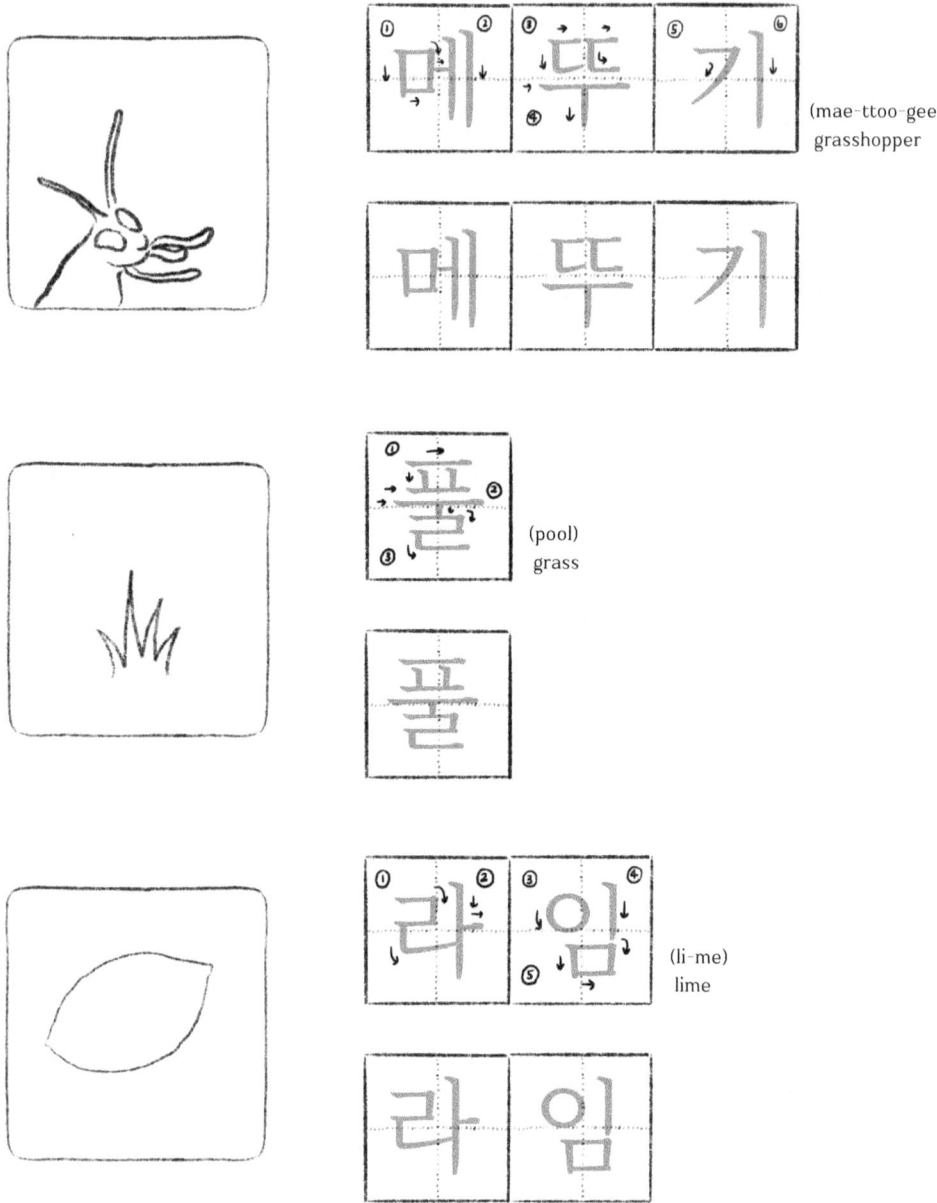

(mae-ttoo-gee)
grasshopper

(pool)
grass

(li-me)
lime

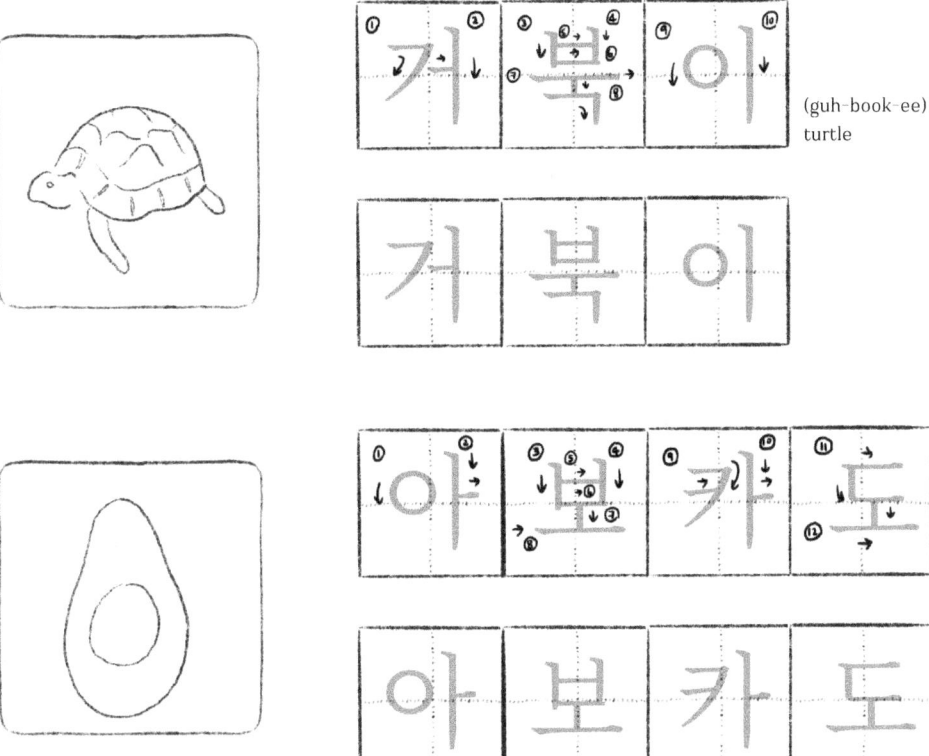

거 북 이

(guh-book-ee)
turtle

아 보 카 도

(a-vo-ca-do)
avocado

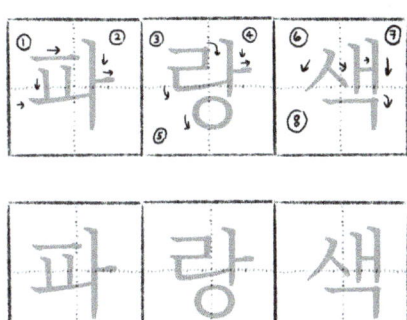

(paah-raang-saek)
blue

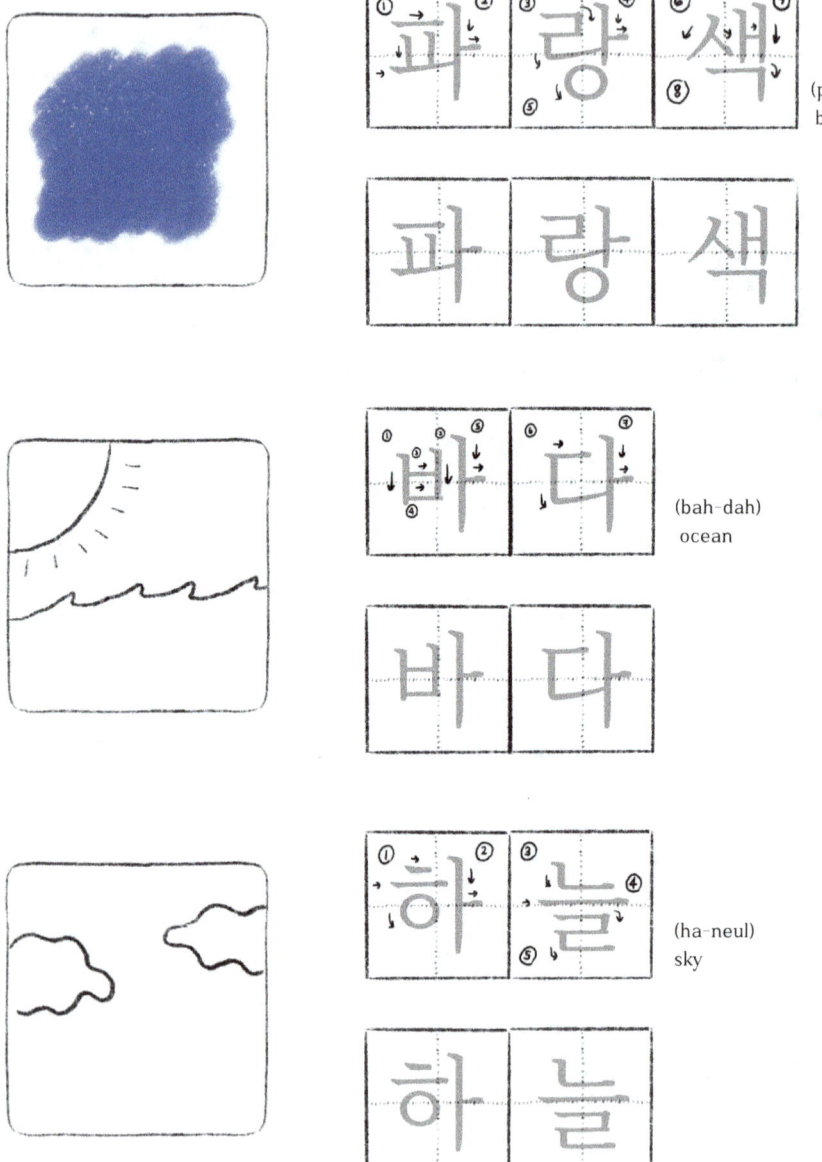

파 랑 색
(paah-raang-saek)
blue

파 랑 색

바 다
(bah-dah)
ocean

바 다

하 늘
(ha-neul)
sky

하 늘

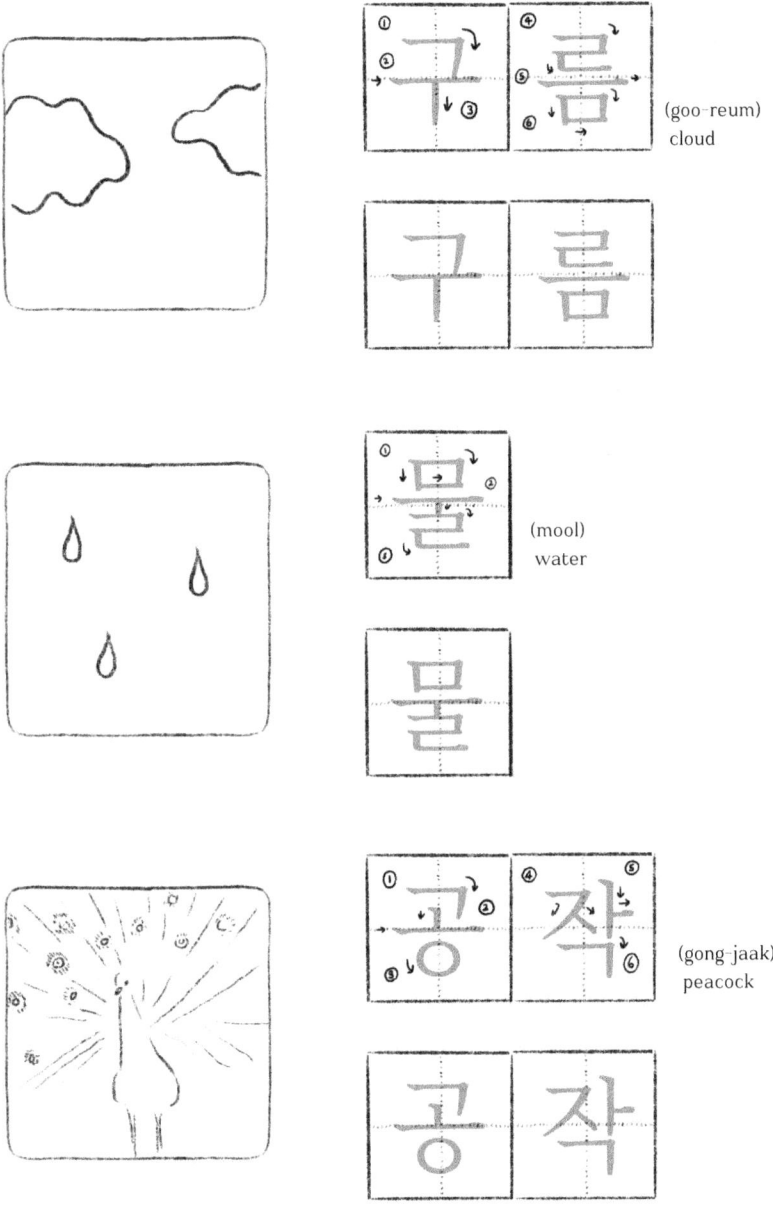

(goo-reum)
cloud

(mool)
water

(gong-jaak)
peacock

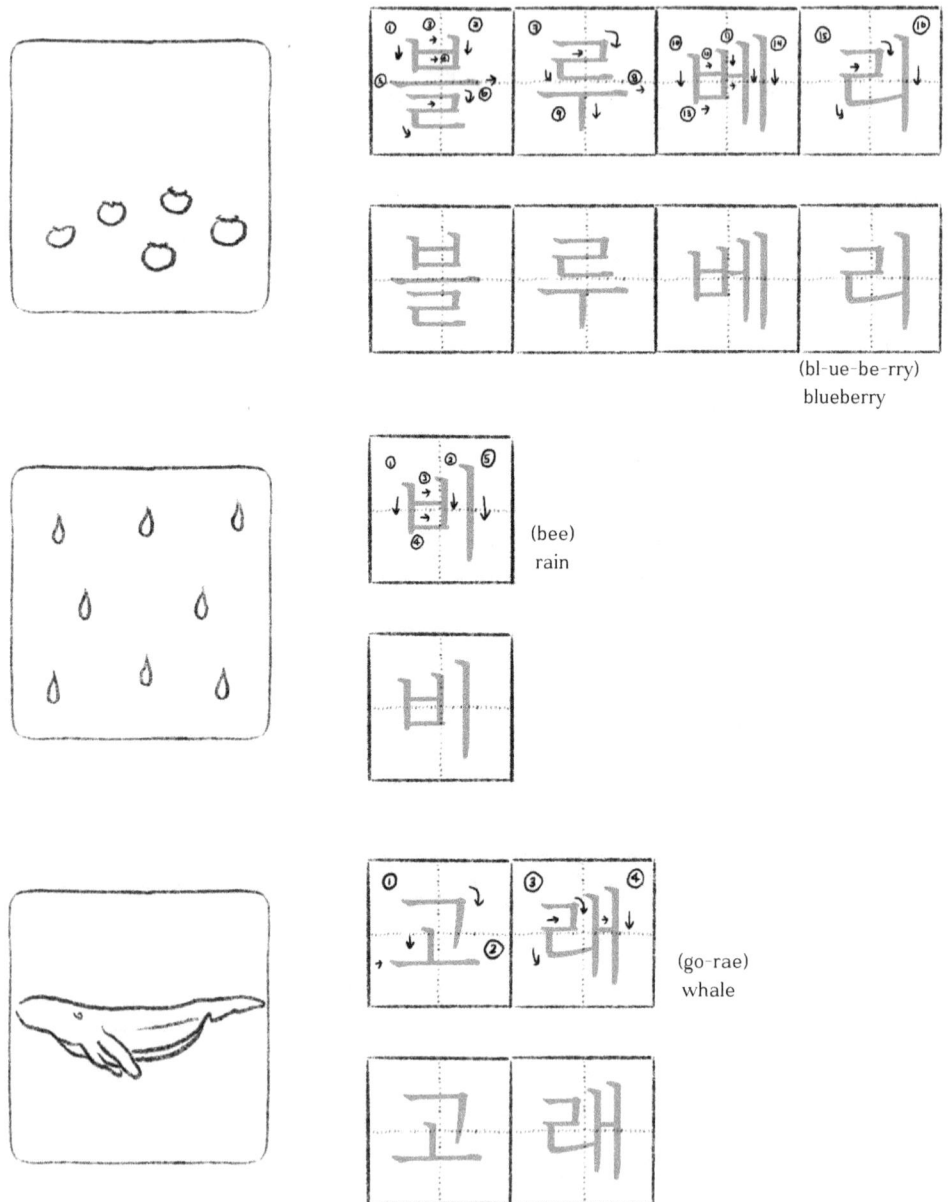

블루베리
(bl-ue-be-rry)
blueberry

비
(bee)
rain

고래
(go-rae)
whale

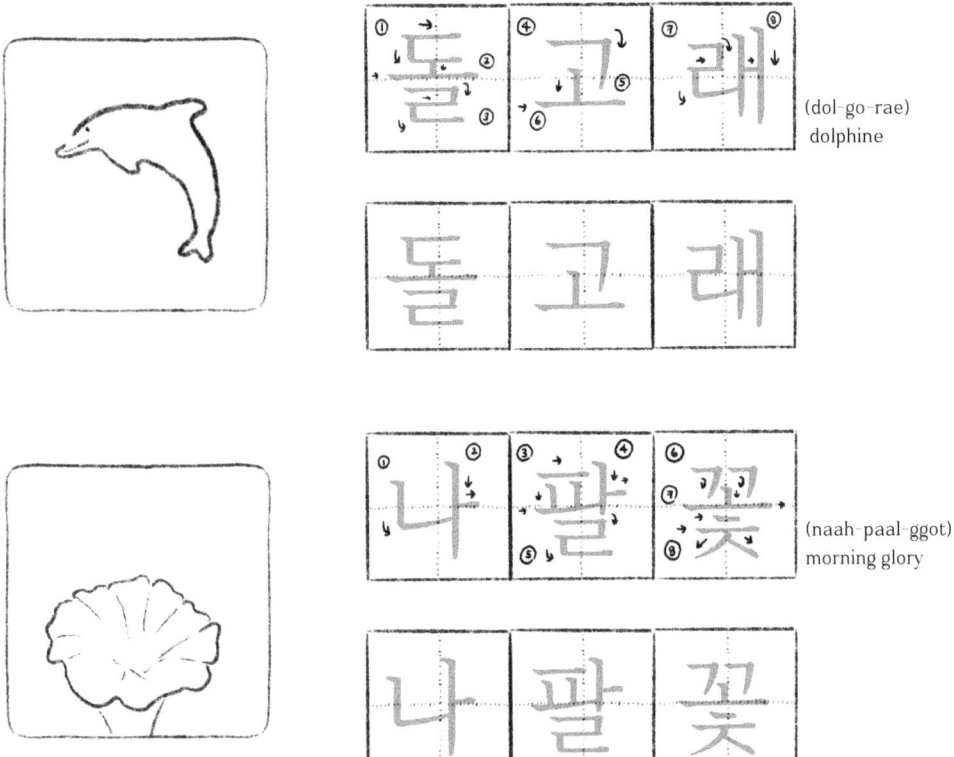

돌고래 (dol-go-rae) dolphine

나팔꽃 (naah-paal-ggot) morning glory

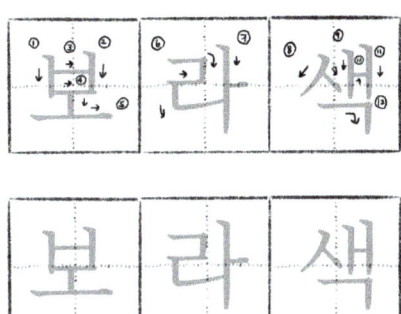

(boh-raah-saek)
purple

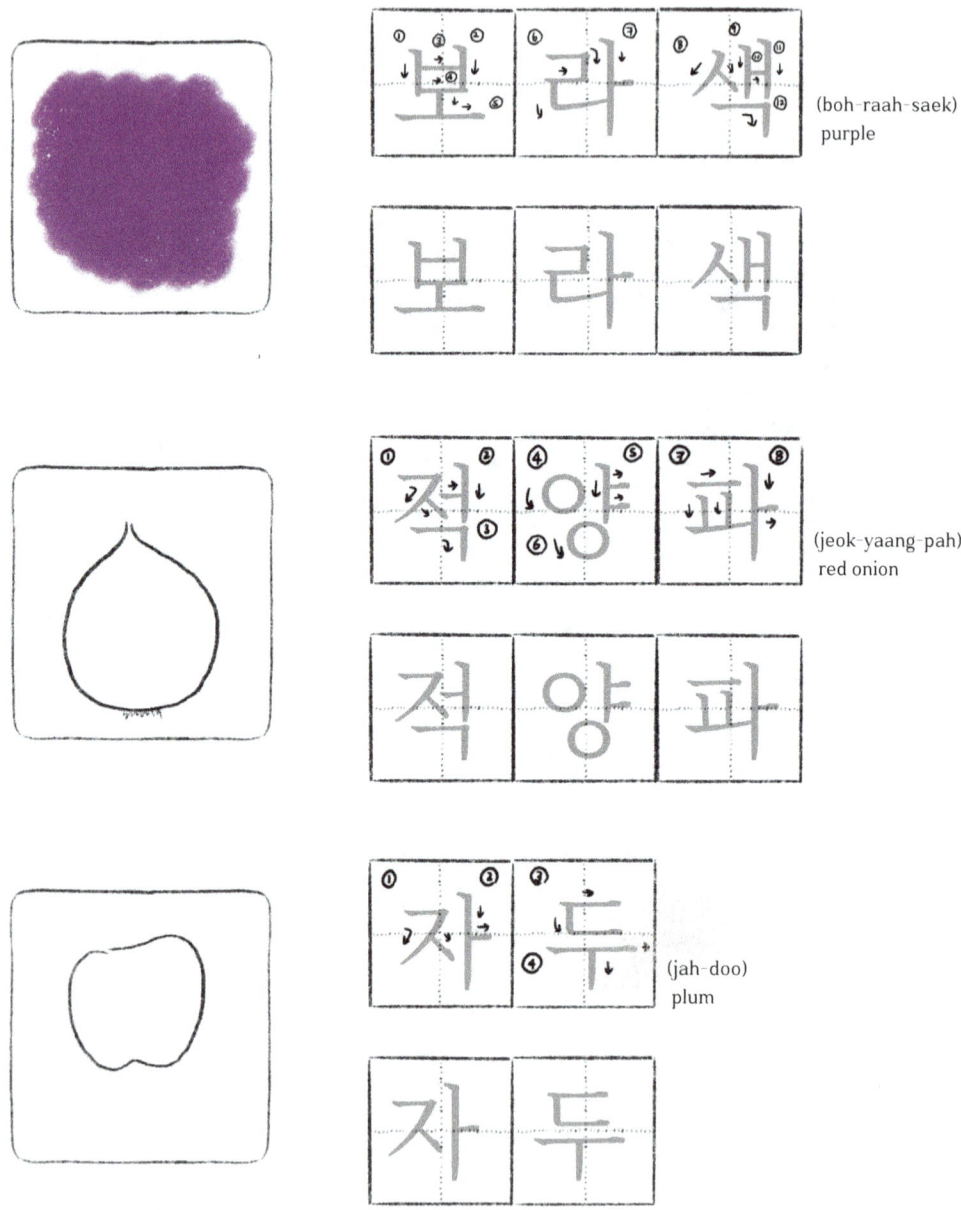

(boh-raah-saek)
purple

(jeok-yaang-pah)
red onion

(jah-doo)
plum

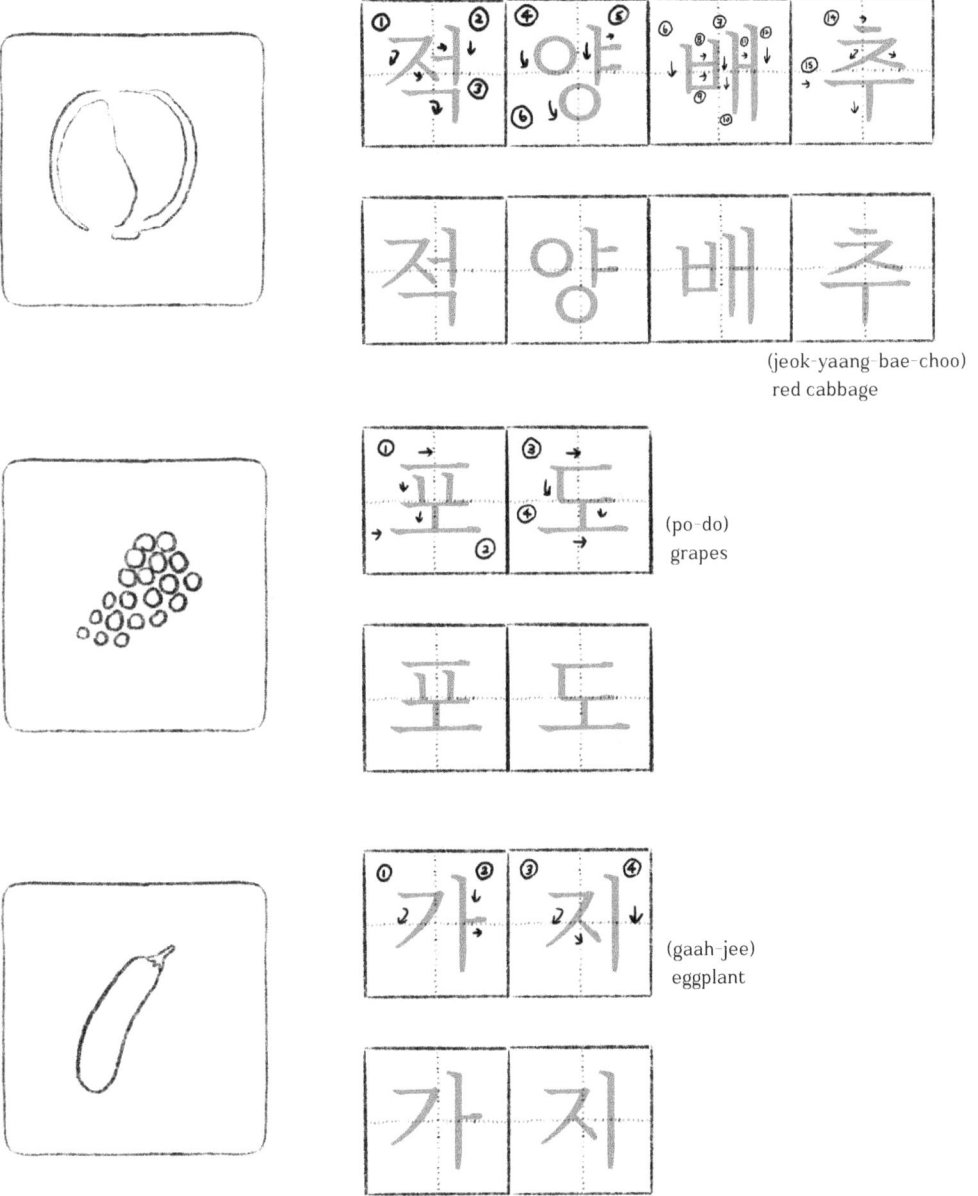

적 양 배 추
(jeok-yaang-bae-choo)
red cabbage

포 도
(po-do)
grapes

가 지
(gaah-jee)
eggplant

*samsoon adventures* ✿

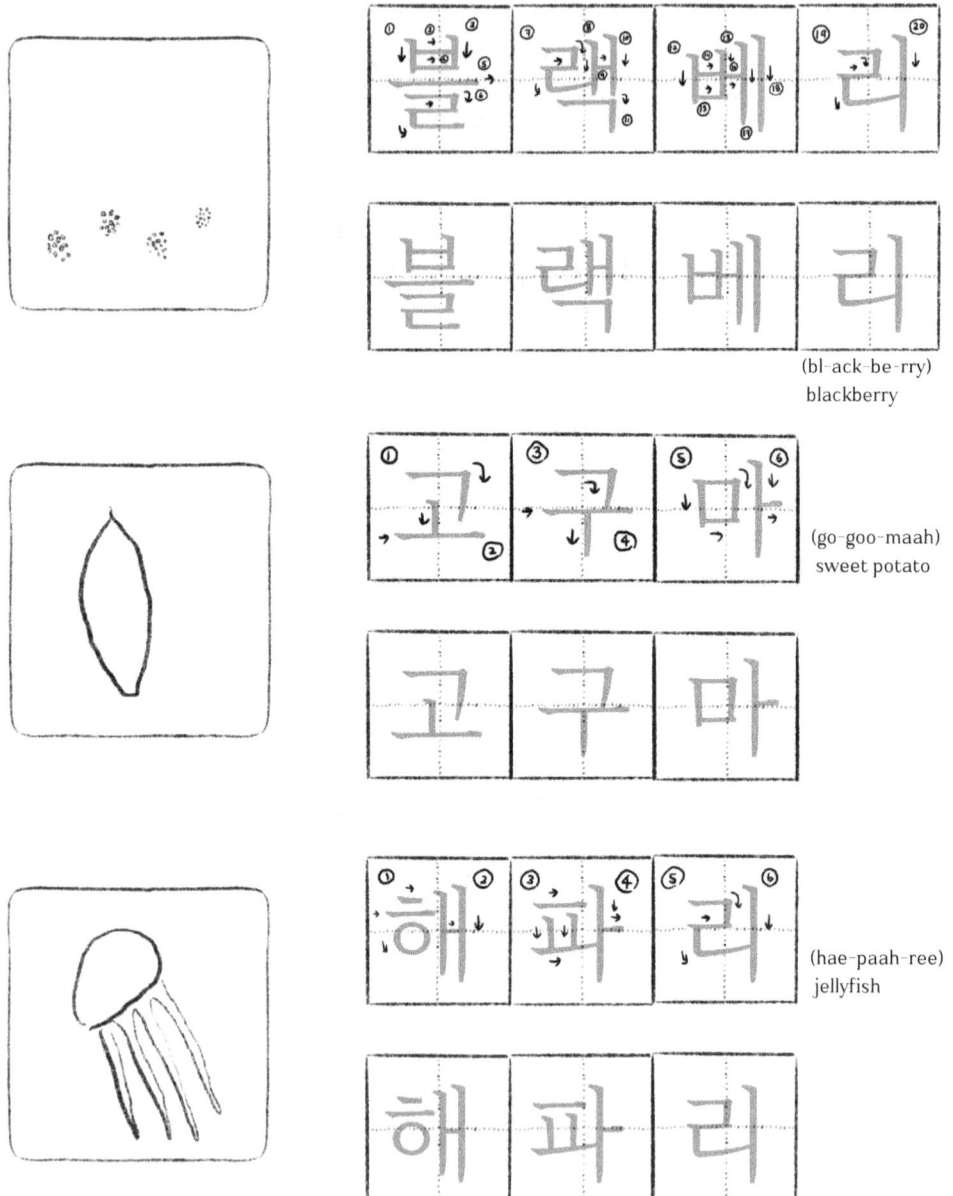

블랙베리
(bl-ack-be-rry)
blackberry

고구마
(go-goo-maah)
sweet potato

해파리
(hae-paah-ree)
jellyfish

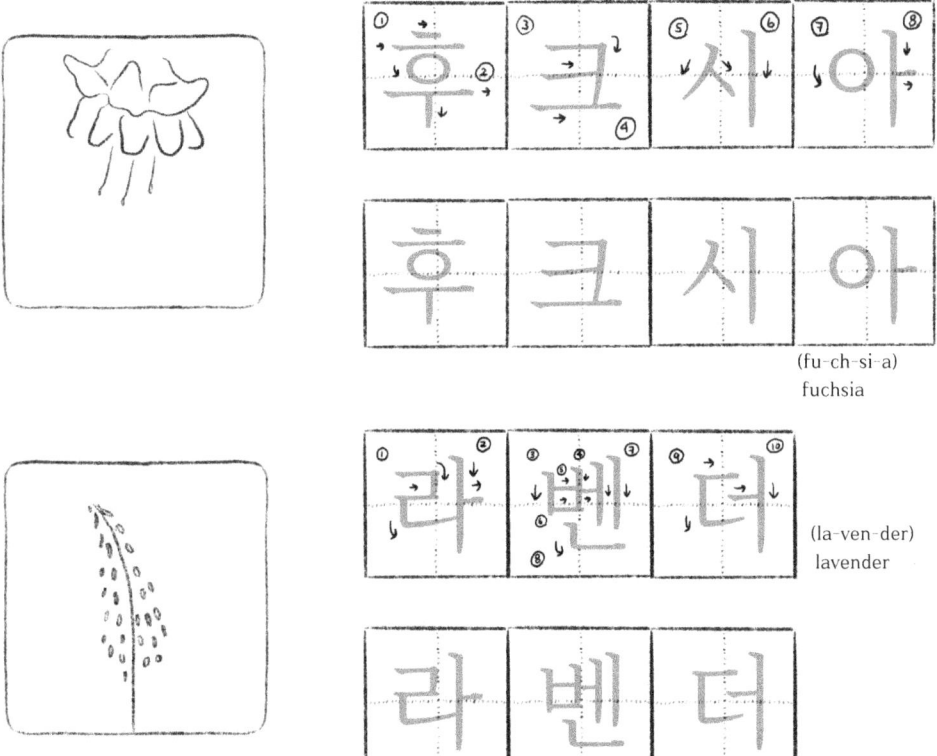

후 크 시 아

(fu-ch-si-a)
fuchsia

라 벤 더

(la-ven-der)
lavender

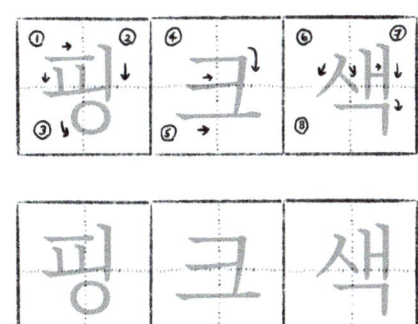

(pi-nk-saek)
pink

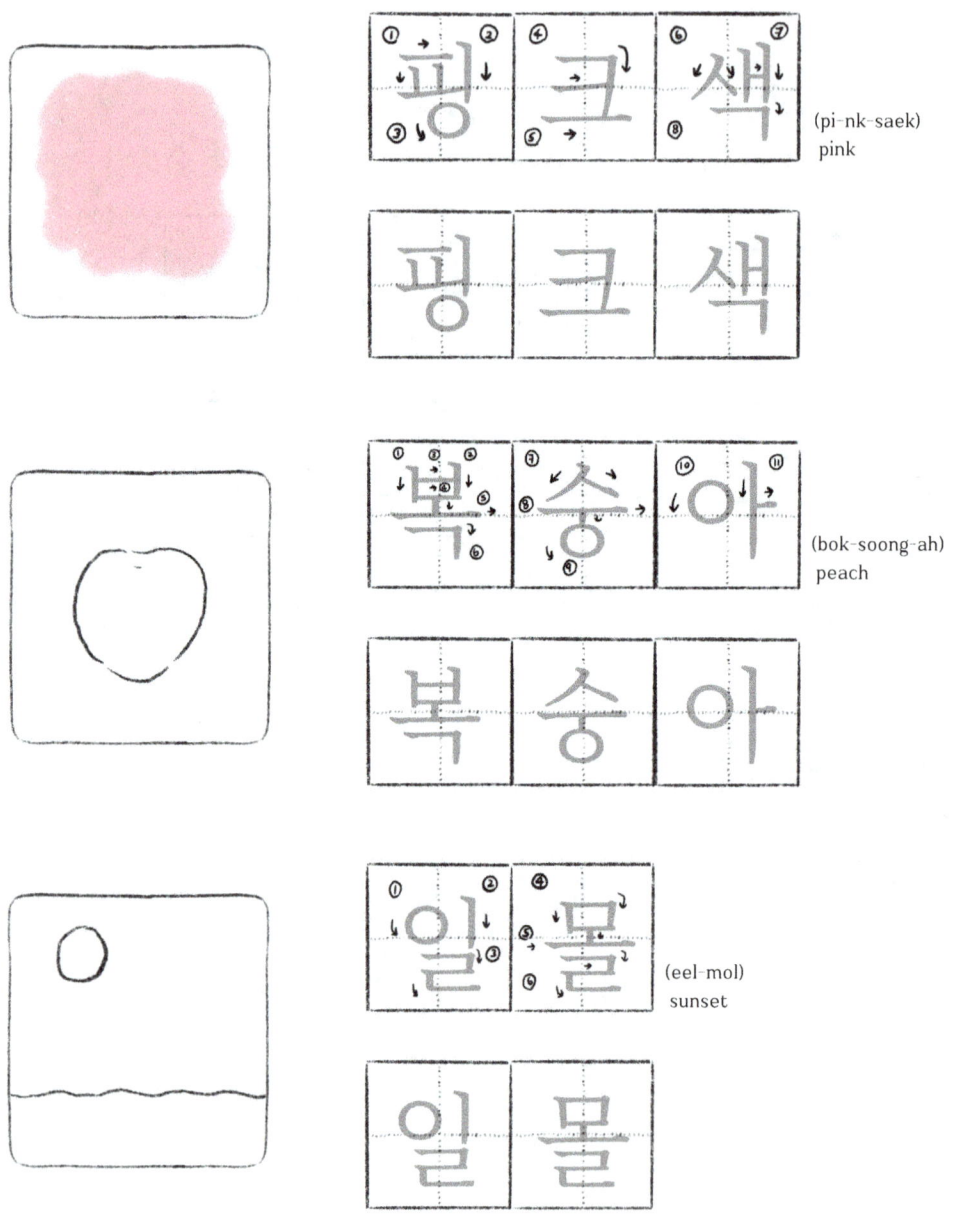

핑크색 (pi-nk-saek) pink

복숭아 (bok-soong-ah) peach

일몰 (eel-mol) sunset

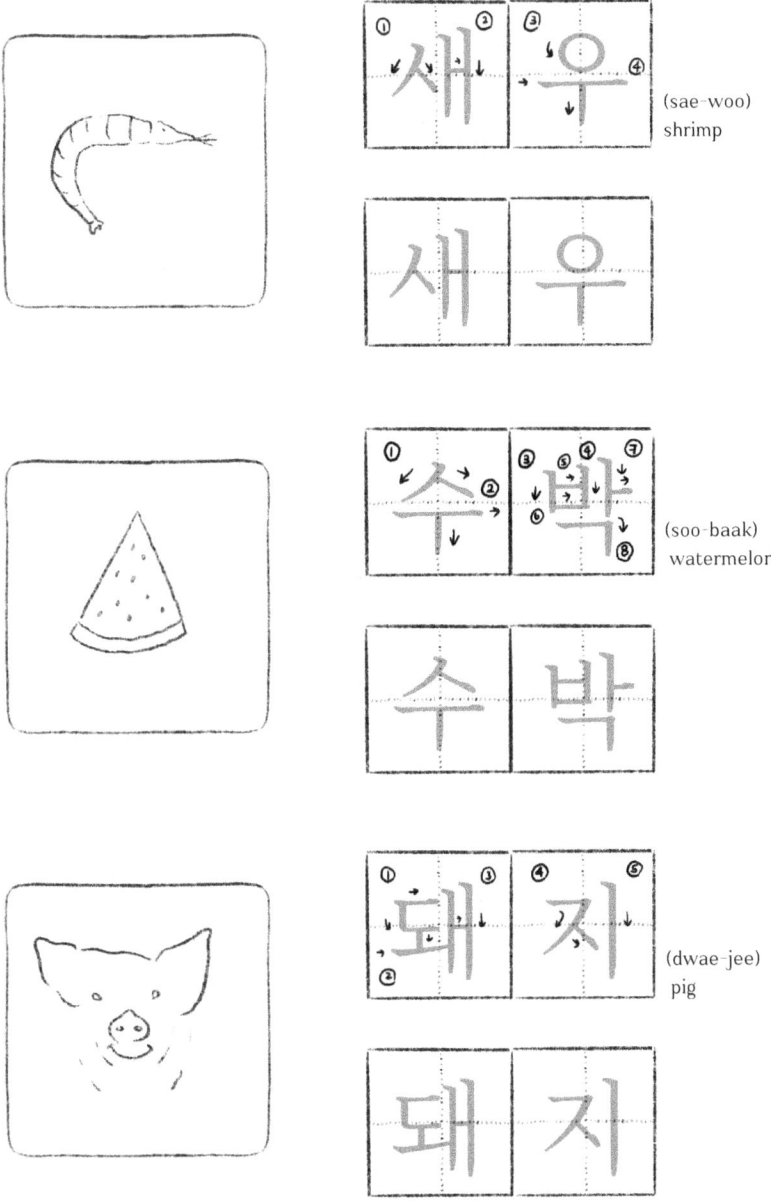

(sae-woo)
shrimp

새 우

(soo-baak)
watermelon

수 박

(dwae-jee)
pig

돼 지

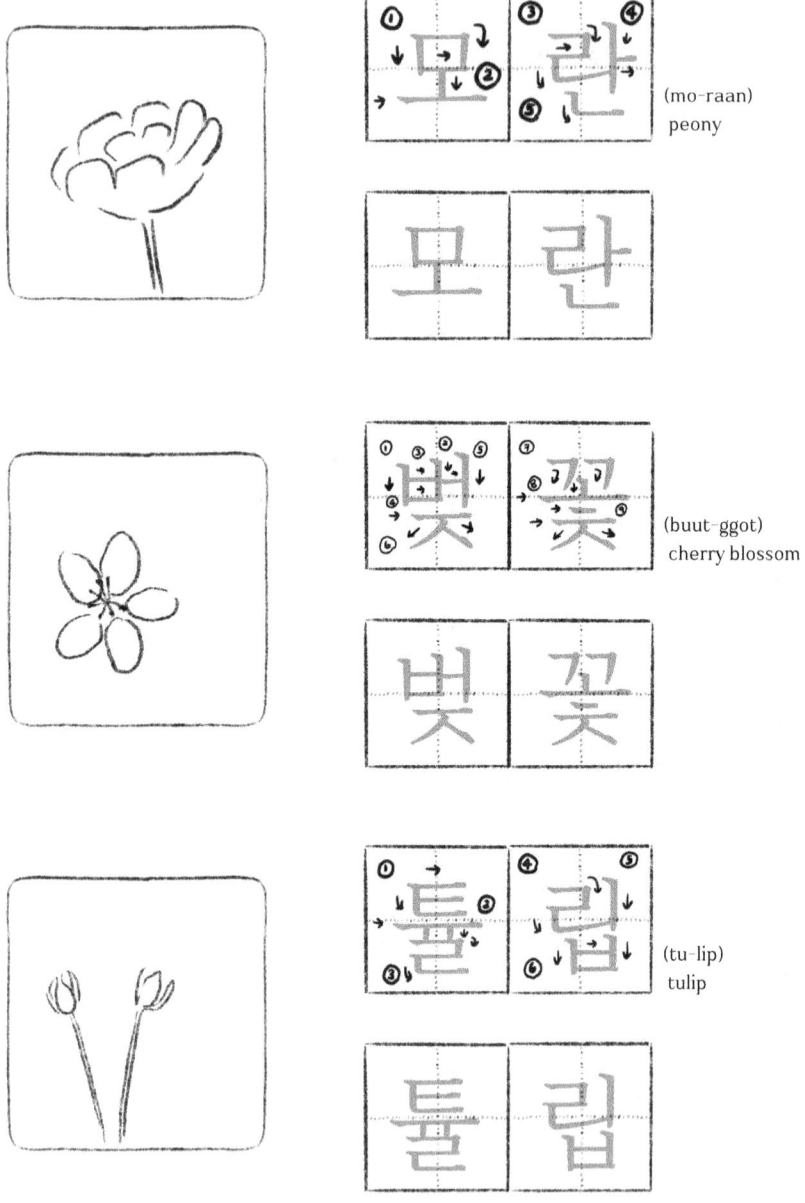

모 란 (mo-raan)
peony

벚 꽃 (buut-ggot)
cherry blossom

튤 립 (tu-lip)
tulip

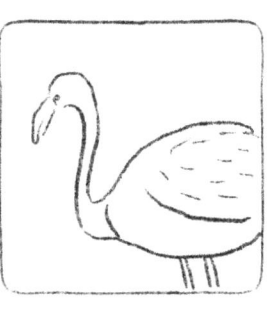

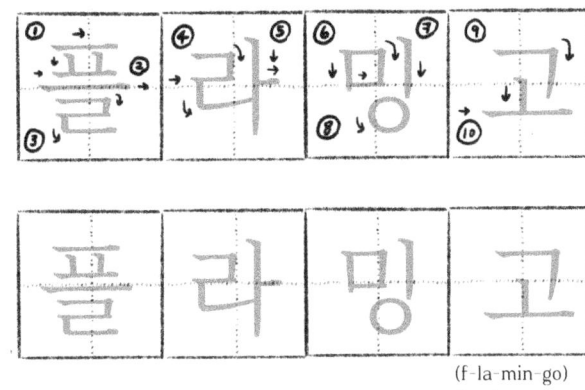

플 | 라 | 밍 | 고

(f-la-min-go)
flamingo

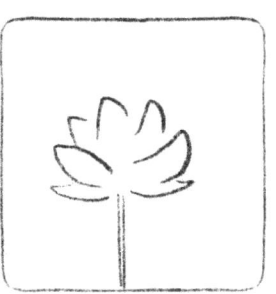

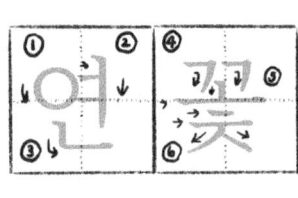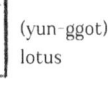

(yun-ggot)
lotus

연 | 꽃

samsoon adventures ❀

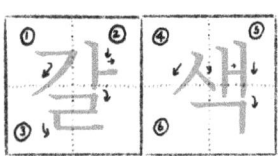

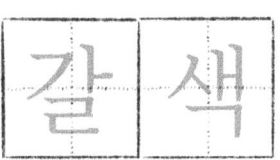

(gaal-saek)
brown

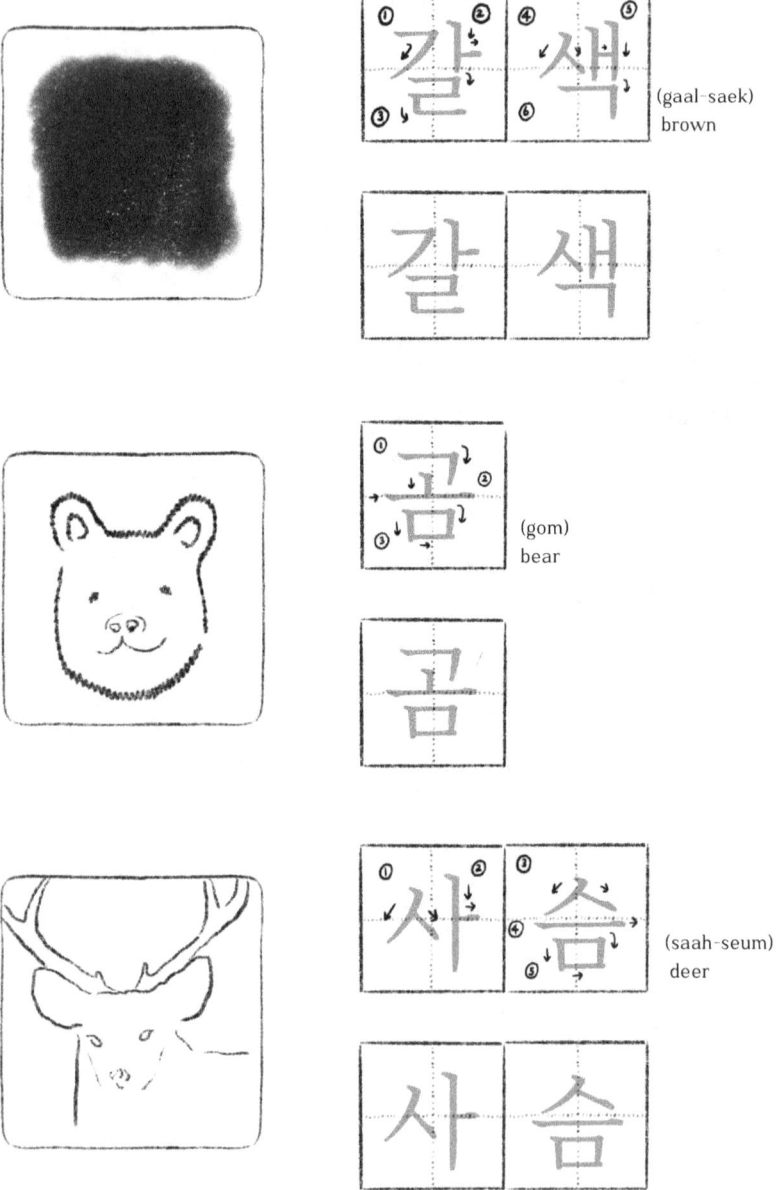

갈색 (gaal-saek) brown

곰 (gom) bear

사슴 (saah-seum) deer

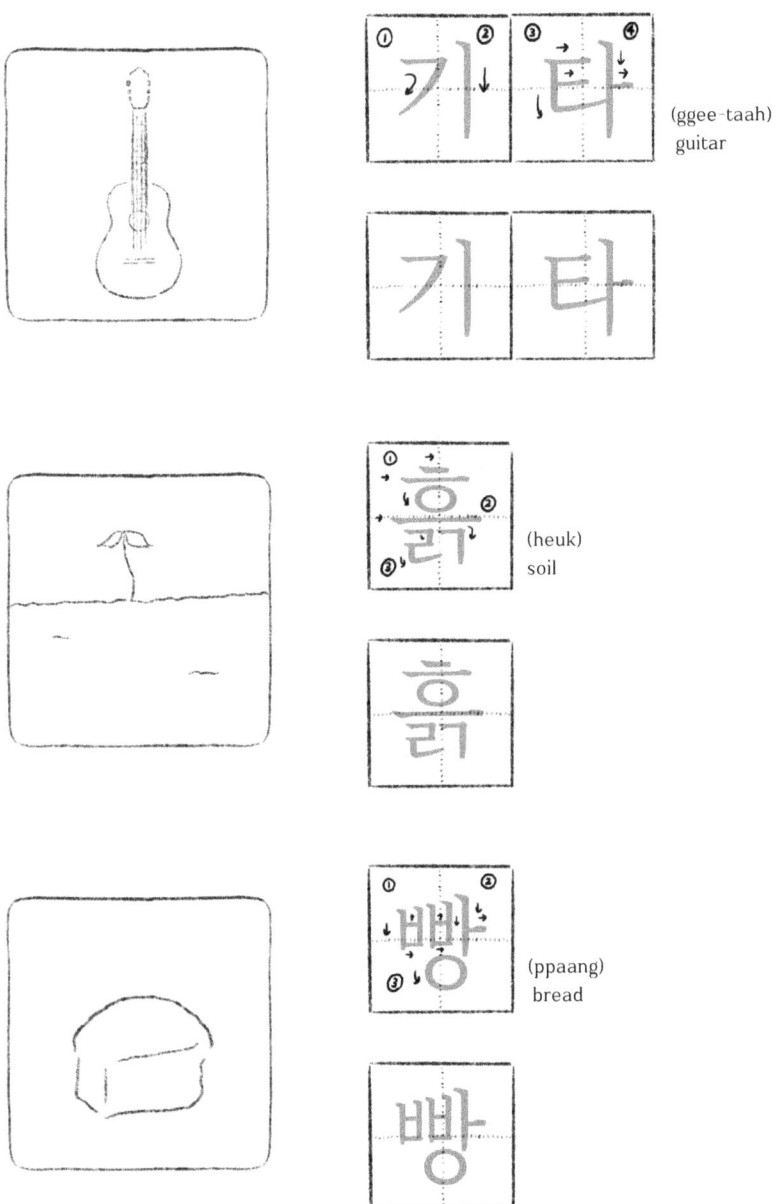

(ggee-taah)
guitar

(heuk)
soil

(ppaang)
bread

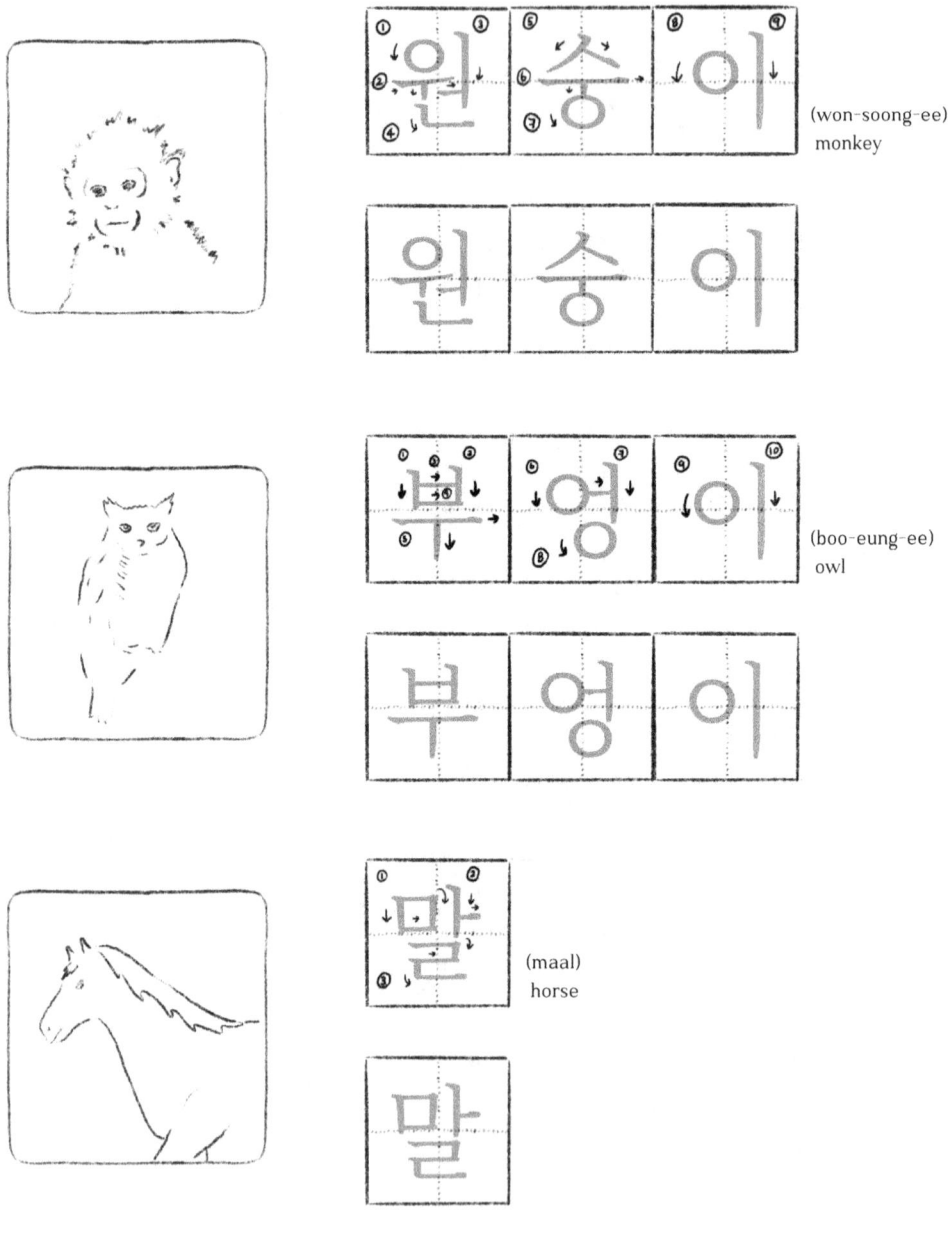

(won-soong-ee)
monkey

(boo-eung-ee)
owl

(maal)
horse

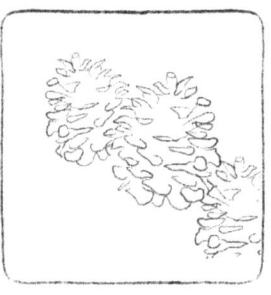

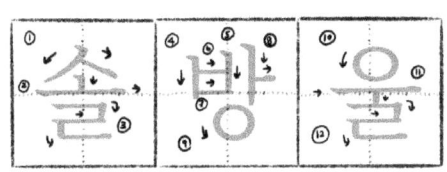

(sol-baang-ool)
 pinecone

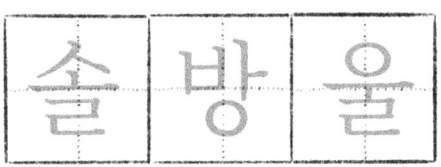

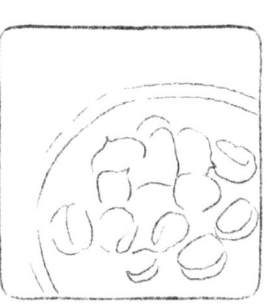

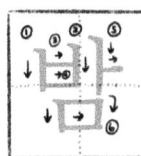

(baam)
 chestnut

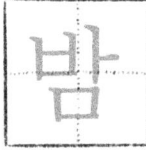

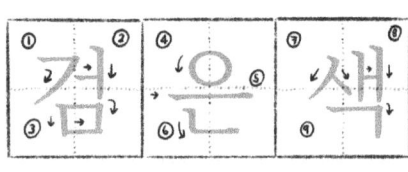

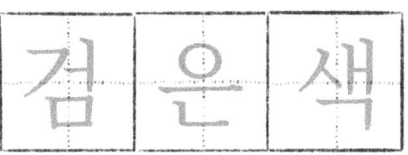

(gum-eun-saek)
black

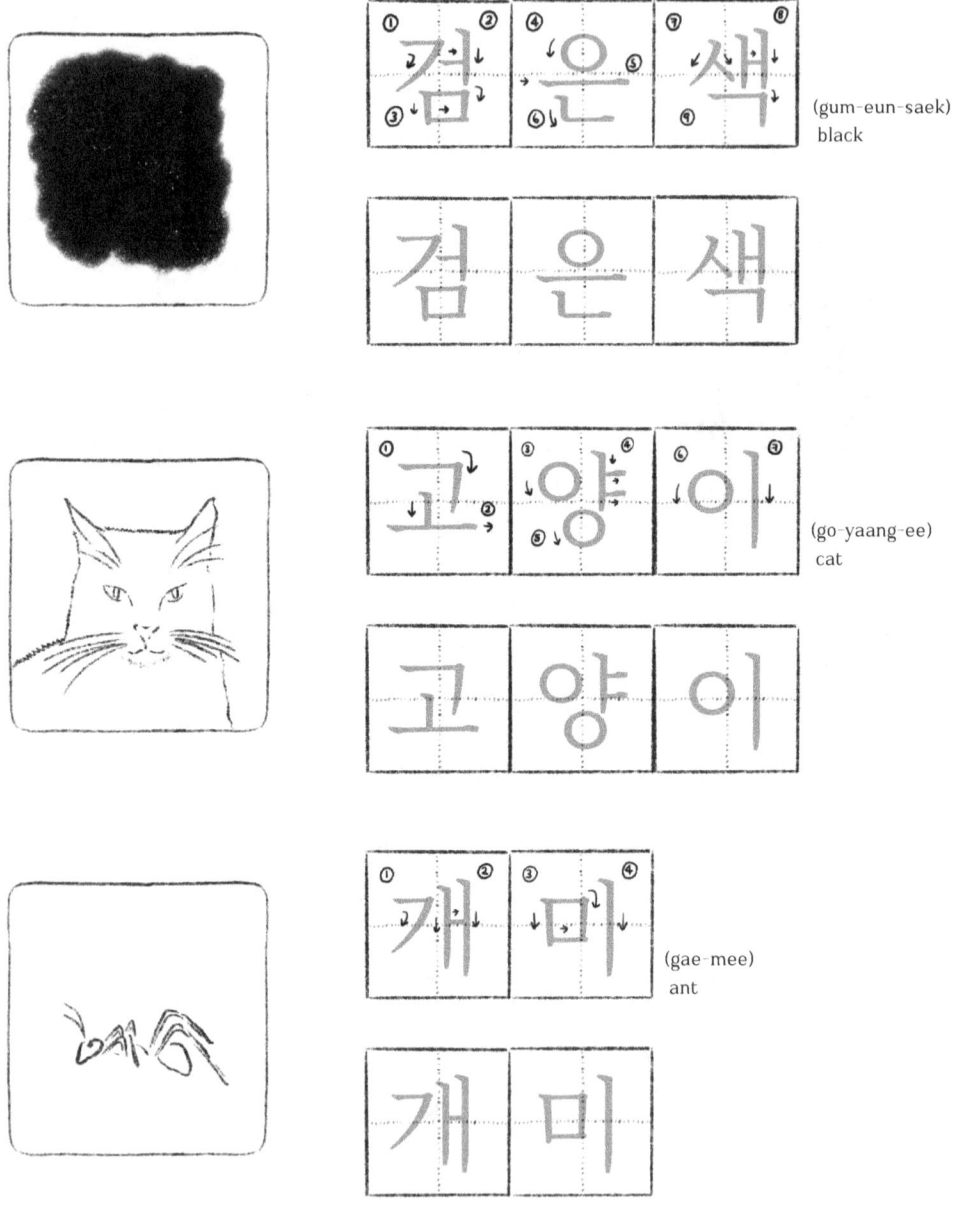

검은색 (gum-eun-saek) black

고양이 (go-yaang-ee) cat

개미 (gae-mee) ant

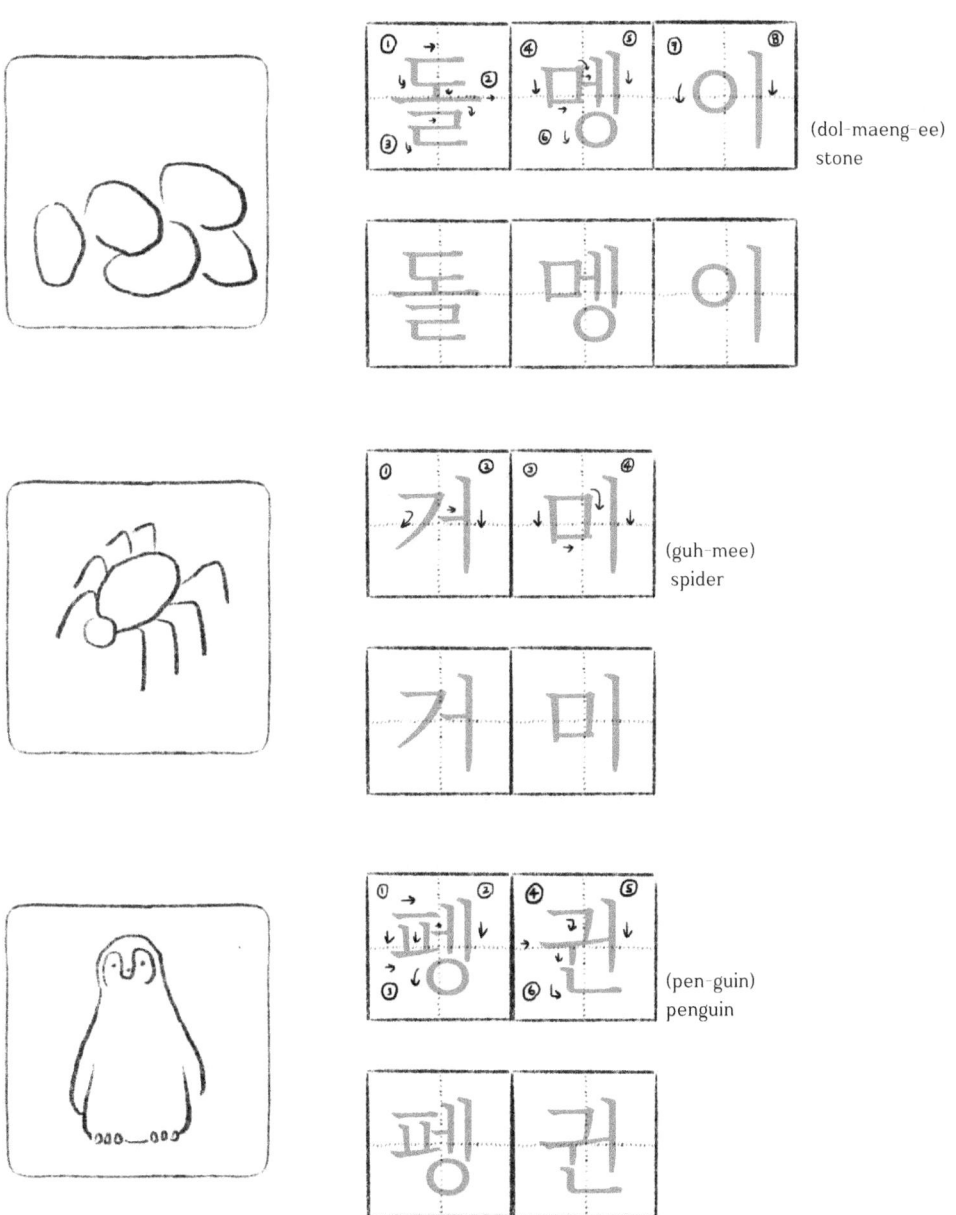

돌멩이 (dol-maeng-ee) stone

거미 (guh-mee) spider

펭귄 (pen-guin) penguin

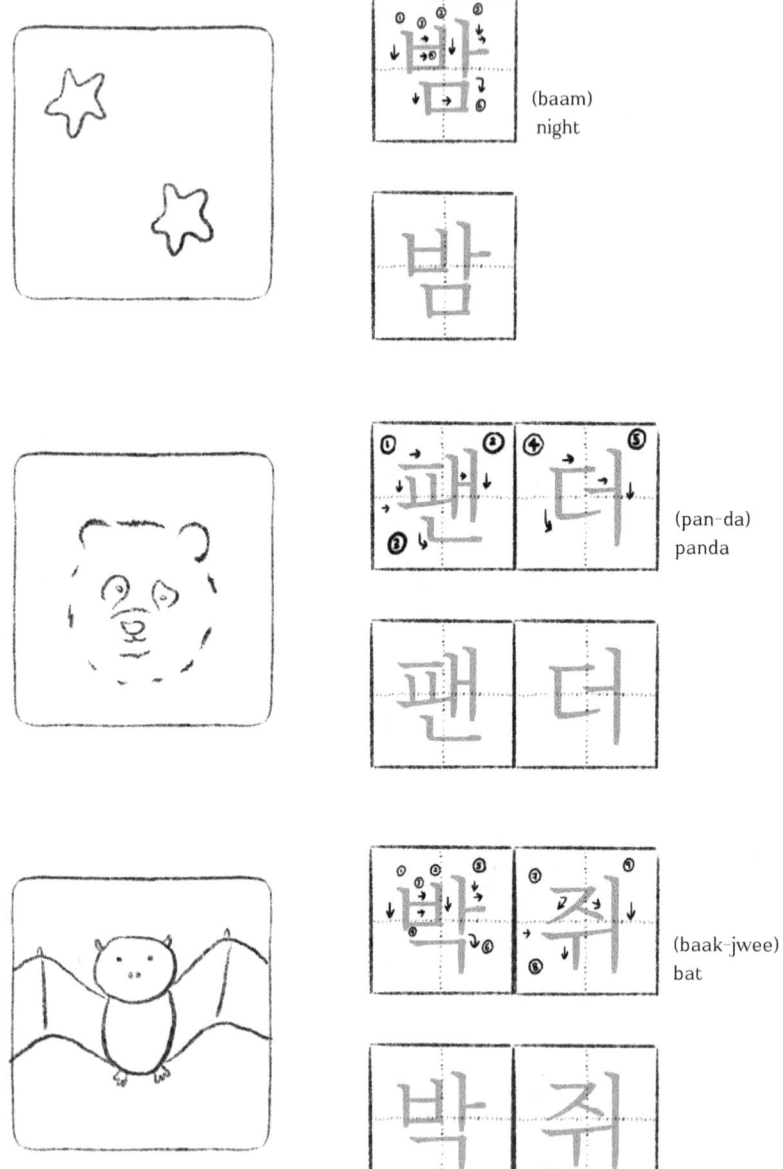

밤 (baam)
night

팬더 (pan-da)
panda

박쥐 (baak-jwee)
bat

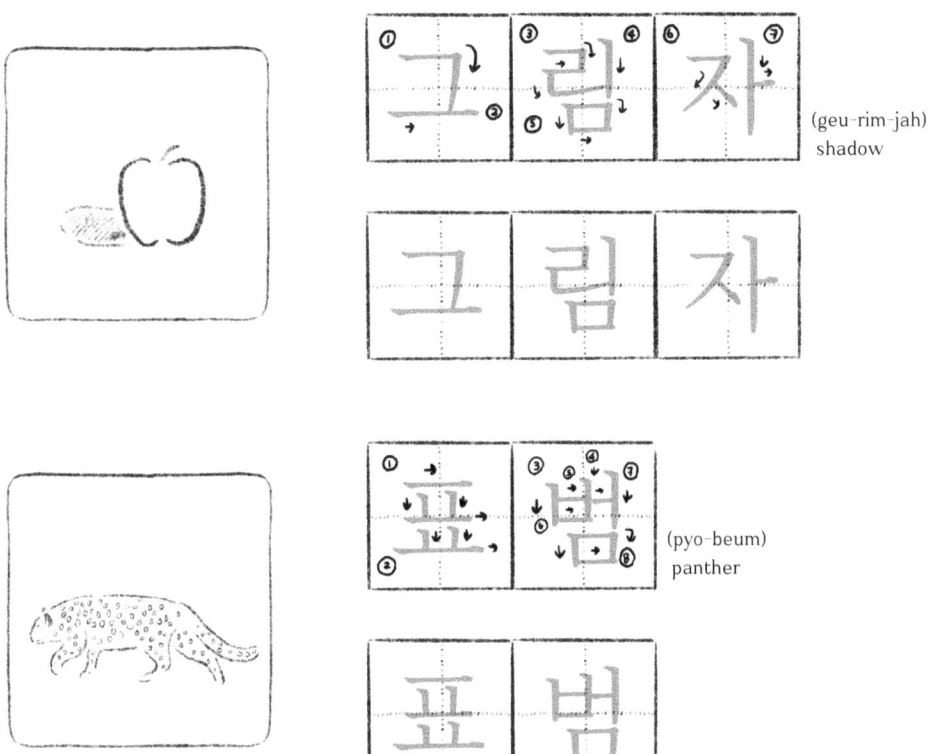

(geu-rim-jah)
 shadow

(pyo-beum)
 panther

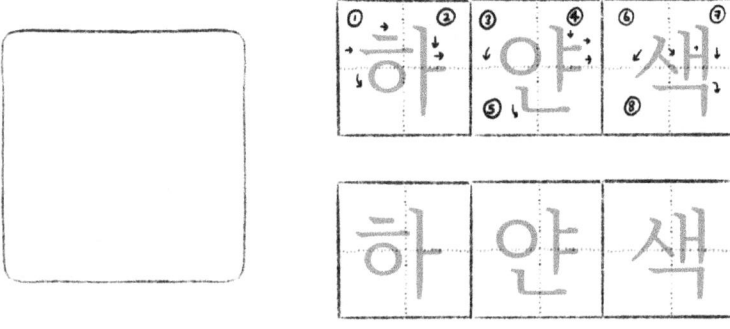

(ha-yaan-saek)
white

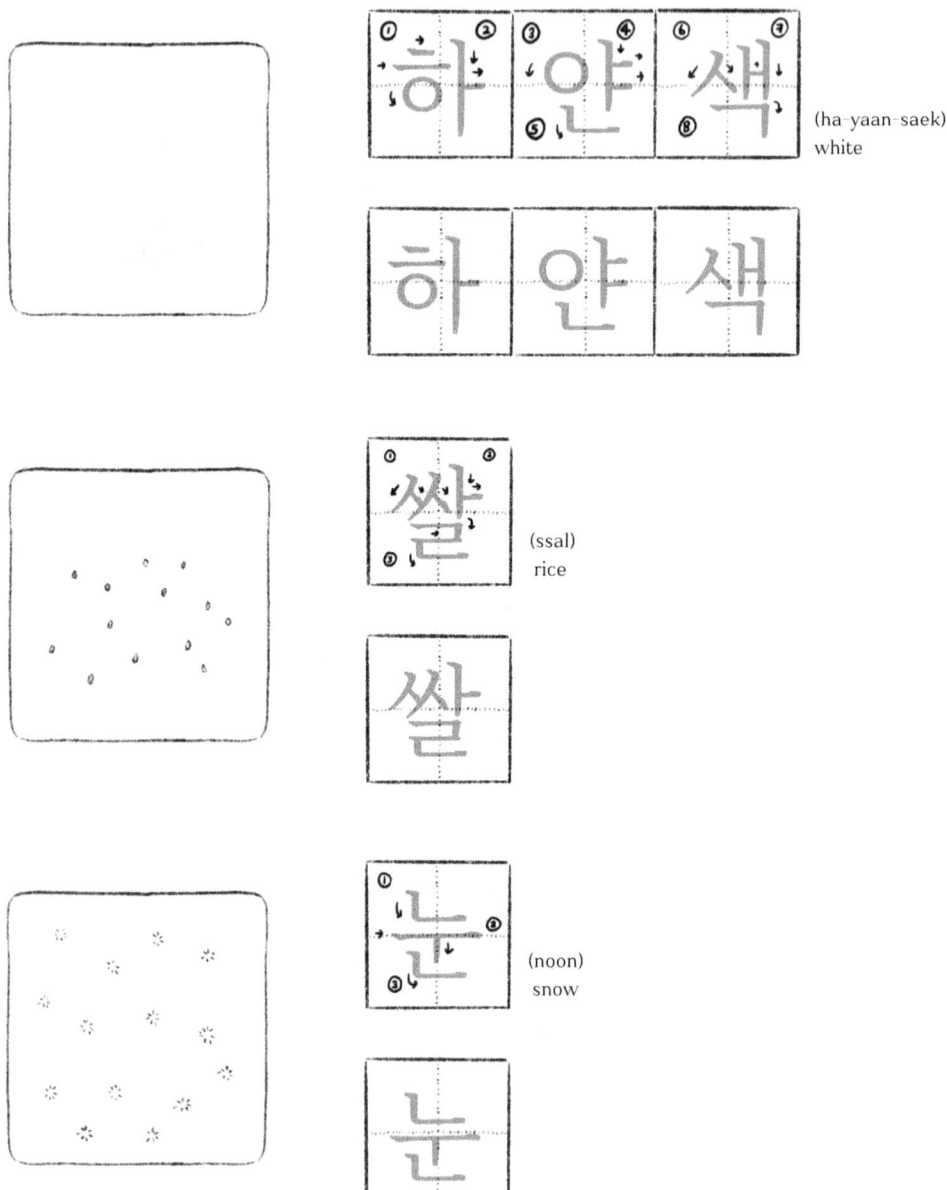

(ha-yaan-saek)
white

(ssal)
rice

(noon)
snow

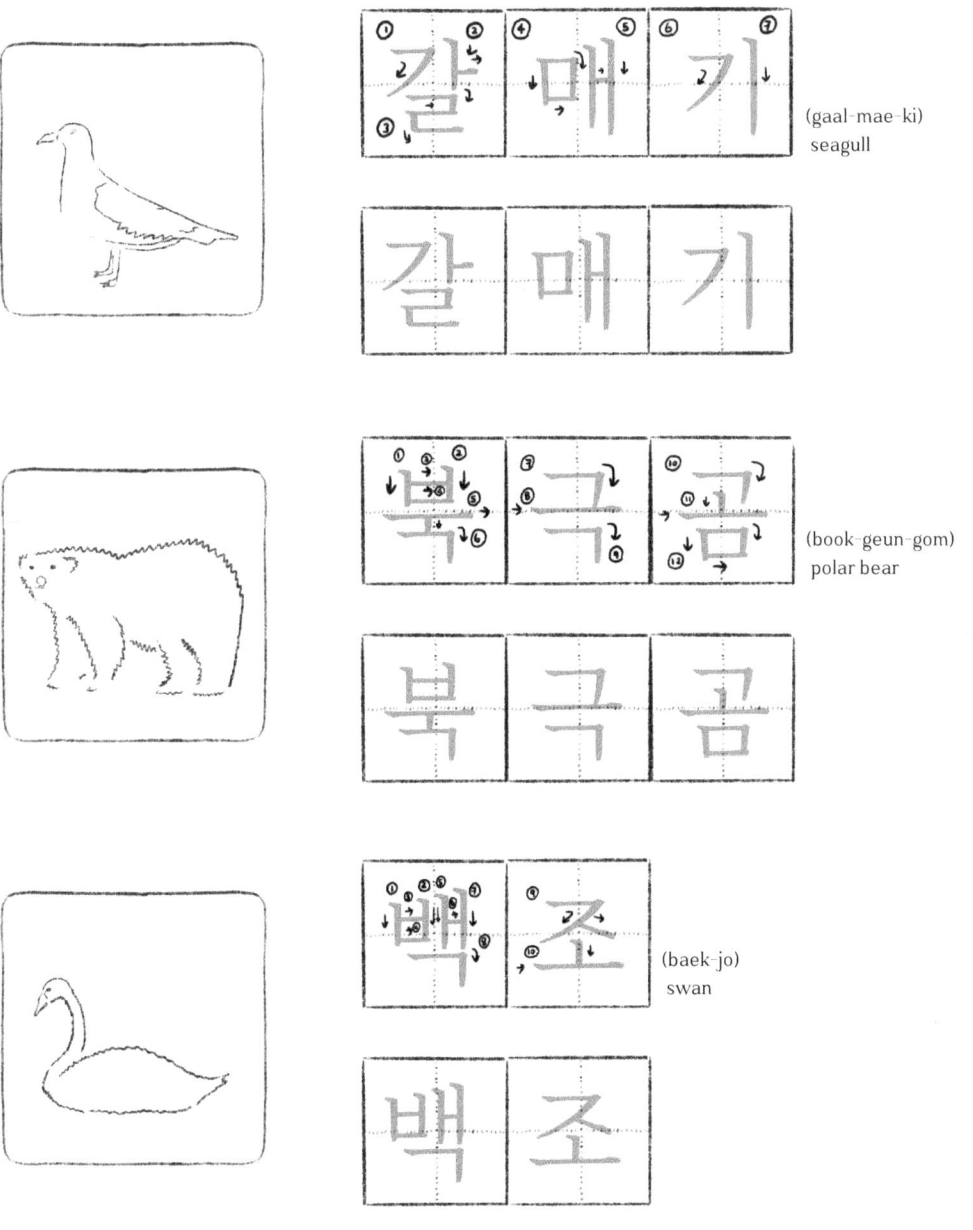

(gaal-mae-ki)
seagull

(book-geun-gom)
polar bear

(baek-jo)
swan

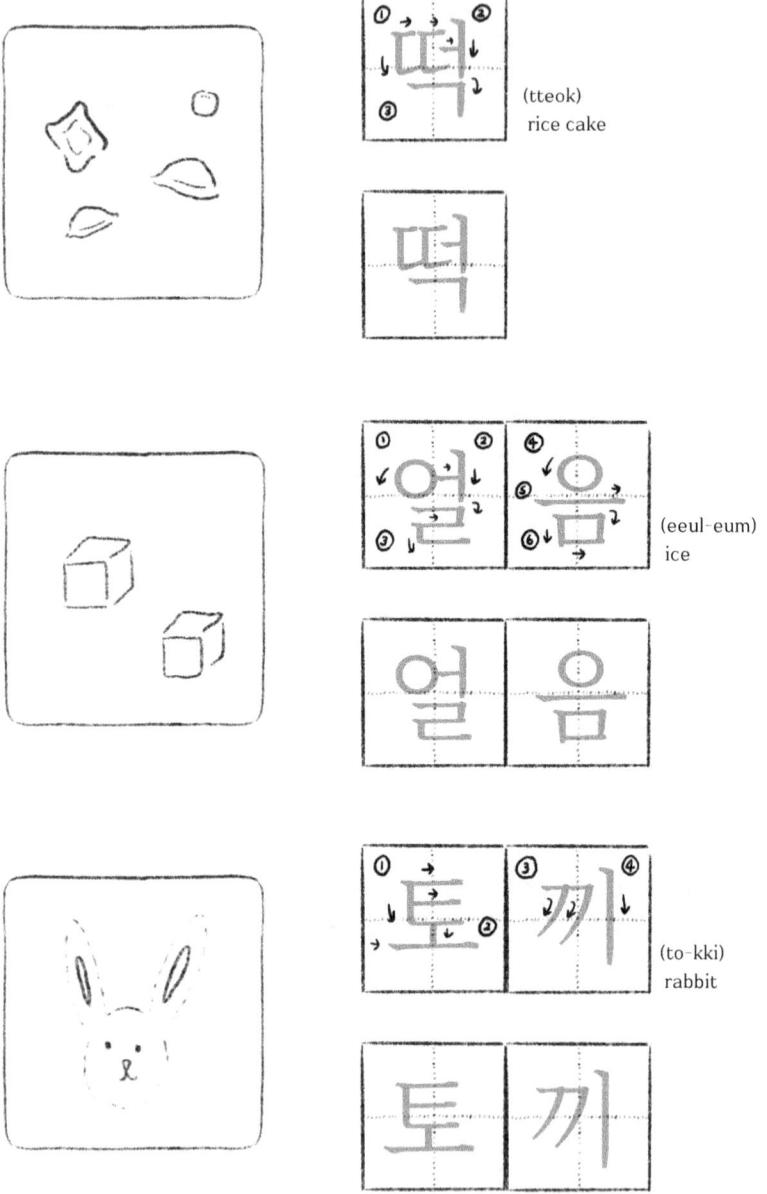

(tteok)
rice cake

(eeul-eum)
ice

(to-kki)
rabbit

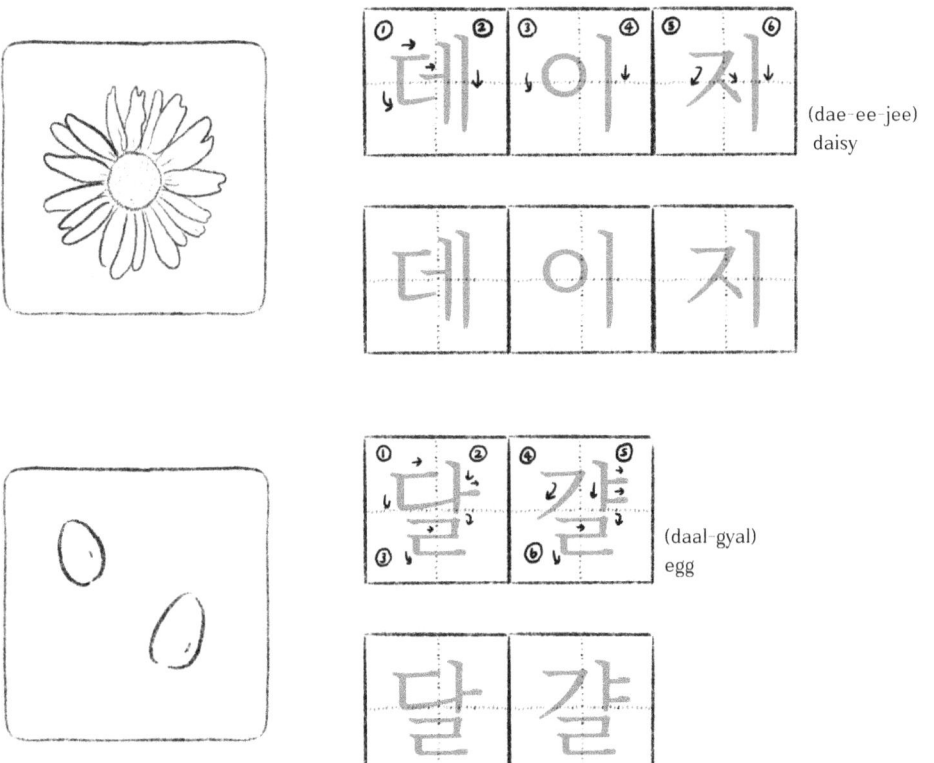

데 이 지 (dae-ee-jee)
daisy

데 이 지

달 걀 (daal-gyal)
egg

달 걀

samsoon adventures 🍀

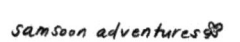
samsoon adventures

# Samsoon Adventures

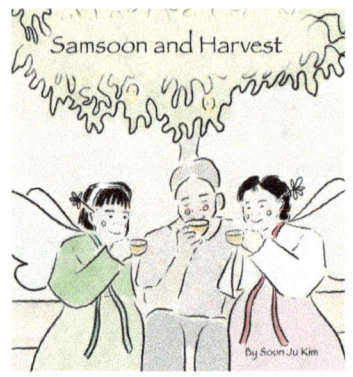

## Samsoon and Harvest

Samsoon and her friend, Rhianna, are ready for an abundant harvest season.

They visit their neighborhood grandmother to learn about true gardening, which includes the daily practice of patience, gratitude, and joy.

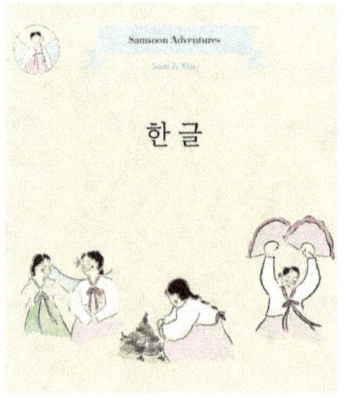

## Korean Learning & Coloring (Volume 1)

Practice writing common Korean phrases, from weather, food, and more!

Take breaks between learning by coloring Korean inspired illustrations.

# Samsoon Adventures

## Another Day, Another Blessing

Write down your self-guided, self-oriented daily to-dos, gratitude, and reflections.

Mindfulness productivity design inspired by Korean time wheel.

Cultivate an ever-blossoming self-purposeful garden! How-to use provided.

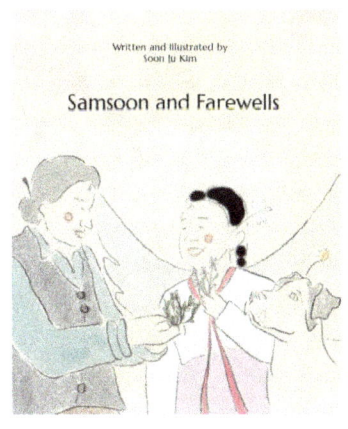

Written and Illustrated by
Soon Ju Kim

**Samsoon and Farewells**

## Samsoon and Farewells

Samsoon and Mimi were best friends, finding joy in everyday experiences with their Grandma.

One day, Samsoon faces the reality of departing from her best friend.

We learn with Samsoon the beauty of departures and how to overcome them gracefully.

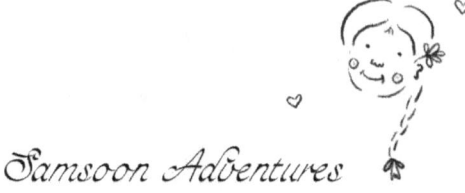

*Samsoon Adventures*

www.ingramcontent.com/pod-product-compliance
Lightning Source LLC
Chambersburg PA
CBHW070436290526
45791CB00005B/1999